I0470058

SIXTEEN
S
T
E
P
S
TO $IX FIGURE$

A Game Plan for
Sales Success

Samuel T. Foust

authorHOUSE®

AuthorHouse™
1663 Liberty Drive
Bloomington, IN 47403
www.authorhouse.com
Phone: 1-800-839-8640

© 2010 Samuel T. Foust. All rights reserved.

No part of this book may be reproduced, stored in a retrieval system, or transmitted by any means without the written permission of the author.

First published by AuthorHouse 12/14/2010

ISBN: 978-1-4520-5317-2 (sc)
ISBN: 978-1-4520-5318-9 (dj)
ISBN: 978-1-4520-5319-6 (e)

Library of Congress Control Number: 2010918654

Printed in the United States of America

Any people depicted in stock imagery provided by Thinkstock are models, and such images are being used for illustrative purposes only.
Certain stock imagery © Thinkstock.

This book is printed on acid-free paper.

Because of the dynamic nature of the Internet, any Web addresses or links contained in this book may have changed since publication and may no longer be valid. The views expressed in this work are solely those of the author and do not necessarily reflect the views of the publisher, and the publisher hereby disclaims any responsibility for them.

SIXTEEN STEPS TO $IX-FIGURE$:
A GAME PLAN FOR SALES SUCCESS

Samuel T. Foust

This book is dedicated to my son Andrew – and also to all who work in the retail automotive industry and DO NOT own a plaid jacket.

TABLE OF CONTENTS

FOREWORD

I once called my "hottest" prospect only to be informed that her kitchen had suffered spontaneous combustion the previous evening. "I'm sure you'll understand that a car is on the back-burner right now," I was told. Two days later, I pulled up next to her at a red-light. She was in a glistening new Toyota Camry (I was a Honda salesman) with a temporary tag in the back window. I waved; she waved. It was awkward.

Obviously, "hot" prospects become "cold" rather quickly once they can no longer touch, feel, or smell the objects of their affection. Consequently, and unfortunately, the "BE BACK BUS" runs much more frequently in our imaginations than in real life. I believe, in fact, the "BE BACK BUS" ran the last time the Washington Generals defeated the Harlem Globetrotters in basketball.

As professional sales representatives, we dramatically increase the odds for our success when we "guide" our clientele through a structured sales process in a timely manner that is compatible with the consumers' "analytical tendencies" and their "emotional states."

In today's ultra-competitive automotive industry, when we work inefficiently (without a GAMEPLAN) and without urgency, we quite frequently find ourselves "a day late and a dollar short." In other words, we find ourselves making a lot of "ya did!" phone calls.

The best prospect list is a short one. A long prospect list is indicative of too much selling and too little closing. As a matter of fact, too often, our prospect list is our competition's SOLD list. In all seriousness, none of us are perfect and no sales associate closes every prospect. We should, however, expend all of our energies and all of our efforts to minimize the time frame of the sales process. To do so will lengthen our SOLD list and shorten our PROSPECT list.

It is a little known fact that tragedy befalls prospects for an automobile at a much higher rate than those who have already purchased a vehicle. Nothing creates the propensity for an individual to contract whooping cough, typhoid fever, malaria, leprosy, TB, or incontinence like a "car salesman" calling on the phone.

It is my hope that *SIXTEEN STEPS TO $IX-FIGURE$: A GAME PLAN FOR SALES SUCCESS* provides an ethically-based format and structure that will enable every automotive sales professional to dramatically improve his or her productivity, paychecks, and job satisfaction. I am also hopeful that *SIXTEEN STEPS TO $IX-FIGURE$: A GAME PLAN FOR SALES SUCCESS* promotes a paradigm shift within the automotive industry away from "business as it has always been" to "business as it has never been."

CHAPTER 1

FAILURE...
A STEP TO SUCCESS

"Failure is the condiment that gives success its flavor."

- Truman Capote

ARISTOTLE ONCE SAID, "It is possible to fail in many ways… while to succeed is possible only in one way." The ways in which a salesperson can fail are too numerous to even touch upon. Anyone who has ever associated him or herself with a retail sales experience has seen sales associates shoot themselves in the foot more often than Deputy Fife as he guarded Otis at the Mayberry jail.

The good news is: the definition of success in the automobile business is similar to the standard of success for Major League baseball players. Baseball Hall of Famers Yogi Berra (.285), Reggie Jackson (.262) and Cal Ripken, Jr. (.276) failed to get a hit in over seventy percent of their at-bats; yet, all three are esteemed as elite members of baseball history. In fact, Cal Ripken, Jr. received a higher percentile of potential votes for Hall of Fame induction (over ninety-eight percent!) than Ty Cobb, Hank Aaron, or Babe Ruth.

It is a reassuring concept to be able to attain success while often failing and being unsuccessful over seventy percent of the time. The key to achieving a successful closing ratio (and a good closing ratio is imperative to success in sales) is twofold. One, we need to be fully aware of our ultimate objective as it relates to raising the closing ratio in an ongoing step-by-step process as opposed to some magical remedy. Closing ratios (the equivalent to batting averages in baseball) are increased through executing a GAME PLAN based on a series of steps carried out with consistency and in sequential order. Number two, a mastery of each step is equally essential if one is to inch his or her closing ratio up one percentage point at a time. It is important to note that just as a batter cannot take a batting average directly from .250 to .300 without first achieving .260, closing ratios move upward in direct correlation to one's mastery of a step-by-step process.

As mentioned throughout *SIXTEEN STEPS TO $IX-FIGURE$: A GAME PLAN FOR SALES SUCCESS*, a residential contractor knows through experience and common sense that he or she cannot build a roof before building a foundation. Too often in sales, steps are skipped, and we turn our attention to the roof before we complete a solid foundation.

Another good example would be to think of the entire sales process as a tee shot in golf. The last step in a tee shot (the follow-through) cannot salvage an earlier hitch in the backswing. An incorrect grip or stance will likely doom later facets of the same shot. When we see our tee shot land in the woods (or water), we can safely assume something was flawed during the process. Superior results are much more likely when the golfer has a proper grip, stance, address, backswing, swing, hip rotation, and follow-through. For optimum performance, all aspects of the swing are intrinsically linked and need to be in sequential order. Is it conceivable that Tiger Woods or Annika Sorenstam would deliberately sabotage their efforts with aspects of their swing that were out of sequence? The very thought is ridiculous; however, no more ridiculous than an automotive sales professional skipping steps and embracing inevitable failure when achieving success is largely predicated upon following a sequential step-by-step process.

Professional sales, and athletics, share a host of the same trials, tribulations, and frustrations. Many life lessons and ways to improve and enhance a sales career can be learned by closely watching successful athletes on a football field, baseball diamond, golf course, or hardwood court. Michael Jordan, arguably the best basketball player in history, once said, "I have missed more than 9,000 shots in my career. I have lost almost 300 games. On 26 occasions I have been entrusted to take the game winning shot … and missed. And I have failed over and over again in my life. And that is why … I succeed."

The point is this: there is a very thin line and small margin for error in basketball, baseball, golf, piloting an airliner, eye surgery, legal counsel, accounting, and/or professional sales. The individuals who pay close attention to detail, have the ability and mindset to shake off failure, and have a definitive GAME PLAN tend to fare better than those who are more haphazard in their daily tasks. Would you feel comfortable as the patient of a laser surgeon who operated by trial-and-error methodology?

Consumers in the market for automobiles are the same consumers who utilize laser surgery. They want, and demand to be dealt with, in a professional manner by someone who knows what he or she is talking about (see Chapter 2, Product Knowledge) and follows a step-by-step plan. As a result of consumer demands and expectations, salespersons who do not have, or do not strictly follow, a sequential order aligned for success can expect an eighty-plus percent failure rate.

Ultimately, consumers determine where their hard-earned dollars are spent; they tend to gravitate toward environments and businesses that generate convenience and confidence. Neither convenience nor confidence is generated from salespersons who do not know where they are going. In our sales careers, to minimize failure and maximize success, we need to know where we are going – and how to get there! When we achieve those two basics – the consumer will follow and our batting averages (closing-ratios) will soar.

Yes, "average" is the norm. Are you a .300 hitter like Willie Mays (actually.302 life-time) or a .200 hitter like Brent Lillebridge (2008 stats)?

Reportedly, Woody Allen once said, "Eighty percent of success is showing up." Hopefully, as sales professionals, we can find the other twenty percent of success, or at least a portion of it, by better understanding the dynamics of failure and success and applying a sequential method to the madness of automotive sales.

The greatest sales strategy a professional salesperson can implement into his or her daily structure is: a proper perspective of failure. It is a natural occurrence that should be embraced in large quantities. In other words, failure will most certainly arrive on the scene early, often, and consistently. If we fail to shake failure off, and fail to understand the importance of inching our way forward on the success-rate curve, we are doomed to a level of failure which prohibits our success. On the other hand, if we shake failure off and utilize the success-rate curve as a motivator, we position ourselves to use failure as a by-product of daily, weekly, monthly, yearly, and career-long success.

We should never forget that a seventy percent failure rate is a thirty percent rate of success. Hey, if a seventy percent failure rate is good enough for Hall of Famer Willie Mays – it's good enough for me. We can only hope our eye surgeons do not subscribe to the same philosophy!

WHEN SUCCESS WE WED

SUCCESS IS PLEADING....
....WHERE PLEAS AREN'T PLED
SUCCESS IS LEADING....
....WHERE LEADERS AREN'T LED

SUCCESS IS RISING....
....FROM ASHES STILL RED
SUCCESS IS SURMISING....
....ALL THE WONDERS AHEAD

SUCCESS IS CHOOSING....
....WITH HEART AND HEAD
SUCCESS IS LOSING....
....YET BEING A WINNER...INSTEAD

SUCCESS IS CRYING....
....WHEN TEARS AREN'T SHED
SUCCESS IS TRYING....
.....IT'S JUST HOW ONE'S BRED

SUCCESS IS A QUEST....
....IT'S SAID....IT'S SAID
FOR SUCCESS IS FAILURE....
....WHEN SUCCESS WE WED

FAILURE IS SUCCESS....
....WHEN SUCCESS WE WED

------SAMUEL FOUST

CHAPTER 2

PRODUCT KNOWLEDGE...
A STEP TO SUCCESS

"We don't know one-millionth of one percent about anything."

- Thomas Edison

BEING ABLE TO display an impressive array of product knowledge is a critical aspect of building credibility with one's clientele. It is an opportunity to stand out from the crowd and the "stereotypical" salesperson. Effectively utilizing product knowledge provides an opportunity to not only set ourselves apart from the crowd – but set our product apart from the competition as well. Knowing the strengths and weaknesses of his or her product, and also knowing the strengths and weaknesses of the competition's product, is an income-raiser extraordinaire for sales professionals who invest the time and effort necessary to be able to accentuate positives and negate, deflect, or overcome weaknesses (real or perceived). It is rare for a sales representative to have the ability and/ or ingenuity to dissect multiple products and provide knowledge to his or her clientele that is, from the consumer's standpoint, critical to a buying decision.

It is important to realize that communicating product knowledge requires feature and benefit components that prove more effective than simply spewing raw data such as specifications, dimensions, horsepower, and torque. It would be a costly mistake to spew numbers and technological jargon at people who may or may not have any interest in those aspects of a vehicle. We, as sales professionals, should never forget that it is much more important for our clientele to be mesmerized by the quality and utility of our products, as opposed to how much data we have stuffed in our brains. Wise sales professionals seek out the consumer's "hot buttons." Is it styling? Is it safety? Is it high-tech features such as integrated Bluetooth and navigation systems? Is this individual motivated by status, durability, or reliability (or any combination of the three)? It behooves salespersons who care about the quality of their performance, their production, and the size of their commission checks to probe into wants, needs, interests, concerns, the background of the prospect and motivating factors!

A new mother and father, for instance, may have concerns about the safety of their new arrival when strapped into the backseat of the family coupe. It may also be difficult for new parents to navigate the entry/exit motions of installing and removing the child booster seat. This scenario screams "forget the specs" and focus upon the real- world needs of safety, versatility and ease of operation. How effective would it be to make a presentation based upon a steel safety cage with crumple zones and boron steel anti-intrusion beams? It would most likely be quite effective. The salesperson who can adapt and present his or her product without the "one-size-fits-all" approach will often "feel" his or her momentum with his or her prospects when searching for and finding the "real world scenario" in each opportunity. The competitor may offer the same steel safety cage, crumple zones, boron steel anti-intrusion beams, and so forth, albeit unknown to the consumer because previous and subsequent salespersons failed to mention it, did not know it, did not bother to find the need or concern, or skipped the product knowledge and application step entirely. It would not be wise to overestimate the propensity for a competitor to cut corners or be unprepared. It would be wise, however, to exploit it and use it to your advantage. In the consumer's eyes, the salesperson who accentuates positives and advantages (and the resultant benefits) offers a more desirable investment option than the salesperson who assumes the customer knows all of the advantages and disadvantages of the products he or she is considering.

Many salespersons make a critical error when they compare their product to an inferior product or a product "cheaper" or less expensive than the one they represent. This costly blunder can often be a "deal-killer" in the worst-case scenario and a "gross profit-killer" in the best-case scenario.

It has often been said that the words "never" and "always" rarely apply; however, this is one area where never always applies. We should NEVER compare our product to another product unless the competitive product is more expensive and upscale! We devalue our product when we compare it to a lesser or equally expensive product. To devalue one's product is (or should be) a CARDINAL SIN OF SALESMANSHIP. It is the antithesis of what we are trying to accomplish. We produce more, earn more, and work at more profitable and stable businesses when we build value. It would be wise for everyone involved in the sales process to frequently make a mental note to pursue a strategy of "first, do no harm." Moving forward is easier when we are not taking steps backward by comparing our products to products downscale in price and quality.

A professional product presentation and demonstration is a skill requiring confidence derived from knowledge. It is virtually impossible for a sales consultant to create a sense of uniqueness without first displaying those two traits: confidence and knowledge. Too often, inexperienced and uncertain salespersons engage in counterproductive "lectures" about insignificant numbers and trivial points. Substantive and impressionable points of interest about one's product are vital in relation to how it benefits the prospect in his or her daily life. For example, a .34 drag-coefficient is just a cloudy haze to many prospects unless we use consumer-friendly terminology to paint an image of a quiet ride free of wind noise and the reward of better fuel economy as a result of a streamlined and aerodynamic design. Simply stating that our vehicle has a .34 drag coefficient proves rather ineffective to someone looking for more "bang for the buck" at the gas pump.

Knowing the background of one's prospect is paramount in order to maintain consistent presentation effectiveness. For example, a commercial airline pilot may be significantly more intrigued by the nuances of drag-coefficient than John or Jane Smith. The Smiths' (realtors by profession) "hot button" may be versatility, functionality, reliability and value. This indeed is the very essence of salesmanship. Salesmanship, at its very core, is building rapport from common values, backgrounds, and interests. Building value and confidence in our products and services, creating a sense of urgency, and proving how the transaction provides more (or greater) benefits than it does costs are key cogs in reaching the pinnacle of salesmanship: a pinnacle that most salespersons find elusive.

It is virtually impossible for an "average" or an "above average" salesperson to attain "competitive achiever" status without first developing a working mastery of his or her products – and a mastery of the products sold by his or her competitors! Knowledge derived from study is important; however, it must be coupled with imagination in terms of how, why, when, and where to use it. For years, Albert Einstein struggled mightily in developing the Theory of Relativity. He knew he was on the right track for years and years; yet, he was unable to find the final piece of his puzzle. Albert Einstein persevered. Finally, coupling knowledge with an extraordinary display of imagination, he finalized one of mankind's greatest discoveries: The Theory of Relativity! The 1921 winner of the Nobel Prize in Physics mused, "Imagination is more important than knowledge."

Who are we to argue with the theories or thoughts of the one who gave us $E= mc^2$? Perseverance plus Imagination plus Knowledge equals dollars (P+I+K=$); that is my Theory of Sales Success!

CHAPTER 3

IMAGINATION...
A STEP TO SUCCESS

"Imagination is more important than knowledge."
- Albert Einstein

YOUR MIND DOTH HOLD

IMAGINE A TALE.....
.....NEVER BEEN TOLD
IMAGINE THE SALE.....
.....SOON TO BE SOLD
.
IMAGINE ONE AS MANY.....
.....AND ALL TO UNFOLD
IMAGINE THE FUTURE.....
.....IT'S YOURS TO MOLD
.
IMAGINE YOUR LIFE.....
.....JOYFUL AND BOLD
IMAGINE A LOVE.....
.....THAT NEVER GROWS OLD
.
IMAGINE YOUR PATH.....
.....AS IT TURNS TO GOLD
IMAGINE...IMAGINE...IMAGINE
IMAGINE THE TREASURES.....
.....YOUR MIND DOTH HOLD

---SAMUEL FOUST

LITTLE MODERN-DAY RESEARCH has been conducted into the most powerful asset a sales professional has at his or her disposal: their imagination! Many – if not most – of the great advancements and inventions throughout history can be linked back beyond knowledge to the expansive use of imagination.

Knowledge is an understanding of what is – and what was; imagination is the vision of what could be. Imagination is a quest: a singular dream or multiple dreams, in an exploding universe of millions, billions, and trillions of possibilities. Imagination is infinite and has no boundaries. The late American President, John F. Kennedy once said, "The problems of the world cannot possibly be solved by skeptics or cynics whose horizons are limited by the obvious realities. We need men who can dream of things that never were."

In our imaginations, we can reach for the stars. Upon reaching the stars, in our imagination, we can continue onward to find what lies beyond the stars. In our everyday lives, we can imagine good and find greatness; we can imagine greatness and find levels limited only by the limitations we place upon our imagination. Michelangelo, the great Italian Renaissance painter, architect, poet and sculptor of David, once stated, "I saw the angel in the marble and carved until I set him free." How often do we, distracted by the hectic pace of the work-day (or a cell phone), miss "the angel in the marble?"

It is no coincidence that the great thinkers of all-time have also been the great doers of all-time. Inventor of the electric cash register, and one-time General Motors Corporation Research Chief Charles F. Kettering once mused, "The opportunities of man are limited only by his imagination. But so few have imagination that there are ten thousand fiddlers to one composer."

It may be true that invention and success are possible in the absence of imagination; however, who among us knows how much greater past successes and inventions could have been (and been a catalyst for additional successes and inventions), if vivid imaginations had always complemented knowledge?

Imagination does not always result in an instantaneous product, theory, achievement, or idea that changes the world. Small gains and successes today may result in incremental achievements and advancements at some point in the future. Ralph Waldo Emerson once suggested, "The quality of the imagination is to flow and not to freeze." Success is much more likely, if not inevitable, when we look to the future outside the realm of limited possibilities and when we do so with a "flowing" imagination.

All too often, sales professionals (and other professionals and non-professionals as well) limit their thinking to the present and the future. It is a relatively safe assumption that future generations will reap countless rewards from the inventors who incorporate the present, the future, and the past into their works, concepts, and ideas. It is a wise student of advancement who contemplates the following: what was – what is – what will be – and what could be!

In most fields of endeavors, "competitive achievers" are quite oblivious to the "status quo," the "norm," and artificial barriers. So-called barriers are simply nuisances to dreamers who have visions of something that does not exist – and has never existed. Furthermore, the "status quo" and the "norm" are primarily for individuals who are satisfied with, or can easily accept, that which is already in place.

Many of the great doers and thinkers of all-time have pursued paths diametrically opposed to the paths of the masses. Most high achievers "do what others do not – and do not what others do!" Consistently successful and imaginative people, as a general rule, realize that doing what others do is a recipe for mediocre and inconsistent results.

Individuals who exercise their imagination are frequently mislabeled and misunderstood. Using one's imagination is a creative endeavor based, to a certain extent, on a dissatisfaction with "what is." The quest for that which has never been seen, touched, heard, written, read, painted, sculpted, tasted, thought, sold, or utilized is not always, in and of itself, an indicator of genius or superior intellect. The late Dr. Carl Sagan, a twentieth century American astronomer and scientist, once offered the following opinion: "But the fact that some geniuses were laughed at does not imply that all who are laughed at are geniuses. They laughed at Columbus, they laughed at Fulton, they laughed at the Wright Brothers. But they also laughed at Bozo the Clown."

In the twenty-first century, who will be the next Christopher Columbus, Jonas Salk, Henry Ford, Benjamin Franklin, Thomas Edison, Walt Disney, or Albert Einstein? Who, in the twenty-first century will see "the angel in the marble?" Who will cure cancer? Who will find new and innovative ways to increase human longevity and/or quality of life? Who will find new ways to usher in new and higher standards of productivity into business and industry? Who will seek the unsought?

There is little beyond the "norm" that we can accomplish until we "believe." To believe is to open the door to our imagination. We must believe in ourselves; we must believe in the power and potential of building from all we know.

What does the future hold? We can only imagine – and then pursue the imagined!

CHAPTER 4

WORDS…
A STEP TO SUCCESS

"Men of few words are the best men."
                    - William Shakespeare

IN PROFESSIONAL SALES (and in life), words can be our ally; they can also be our worst enemy. In the automotive industry, on a daily basis, the number of lost opportunities, lost revenue, lost commissions, lost clientele, and/or lost potential successes is incalculable (and astronomical) due to questionable word selection and poor oral expression. Benjamin Franklin, one of the wisest men in American history once said, "Here comes the orator with his flood of words and his drop of reason." It sounds as if Benjamin Franklin once had a bad car-buying experience.

Effective and positive word selection is neither a gift nor an art – it is a habit! As humans, we develop tendencies from repetition and a lack of forethought as it relates to pursuing alternative verbal options that could possibly enhance our lives, and/or the lives of the individuals we come in contact with on a daily, occasional, or one-time basis.

In retrospect, through our verbal output, do we paint a positive or a negative image during our daily conversations? How often do we destroy a perfectly good sentence, question, or dialogue by using a single word that dominates the thoughts and minds of our fellow conversationalists in a negative or chilling manner?

The usage of negative or chilling words run counter to a fundamental sales strategy: "planting seeds" that may pop up in the minds of our prospects when he or she makes comparisons between what we have to offer and what our competition is offering. When we "plant good seeds" (difference makers), they can often provide us with a competitive edge when elimination and selection choices are made. Negative and chilling words, on the other hand, have the potential to sabotage our efforts.

It is extremely important to understand the dynamics and potential effects of lone words in an otherwise neutral statement or conversation. One word, with a negative or overly broad context can, in a sea of words, overwhelm the intent and slant the effects of a perfectly well-meaning and positive statement. This is precisely why automobile manufacturers offer exotic color terminology such as celestial, pearlescent, seashell, champagne, and glacier; offering "brown" or "green" does not paint a picture of uniqueness or desirability. Seneca, a Roman philosopher and statesman born in 4 BC once said, "What is required is not a lot of words, but effectual ones." Seneca's statement is as true today as it was nearly 2,000 years ago.

In other words, we diminish the perceived value of our product when we ask a consumer, "Do you want a white one or a black one?" The consumer can go anywhere in America and get a white or black car; obtaining a "pearlescent" one provides a "unique" opportunity for our "unique" clientele. Also, as an added bonus, consumers will invariably pay more profit for "unique opportunities" versus "ordinary events."

One of the most effective tools any salesperson has at his or her disposal is to simply use less "floods of words" and more "drops of reason," of which Benjamin Franklin counseled many years ago. As a normal everyday citizen, would we rather purchase a "house" or a "home"? Would we rather purchase a "used car" or a "pre-owned vehicle"? Would we be more excited and enthused about an interview for a "job" as a janitor or a "career opportunity" as a maintenance-engineer? If you turned the television on tonight and discovered you had just won the lottery and a half-million dollars, would you be more or less excited than if told the prize was five-hundred thousand dollars? Would you be more concerned if your doctor diagnosed an illness or said you were sick? Would you rather lose or would you rather be defeated? Would you rather win or would you rather prevail?

Kahlil Gibran, the late Lebanese-American writer, theologian, and third-best selling poet in history once said, "Wisdom is not in words; wisdom is meaning within words." Wise sales professionals recognize the importance of word selection; they also recognize the importance of context and tone. The same word or words can have different interpretations based upon tone of voice, context, facial expressions, and/or demeanor. One person's joke is often someone else's degradation.

Ideally, verbal communication between consumers and sales

professionals should be devoid of slang and jargon. The average person on the street may not understand or be comfortable with terms such as "upside-down" or "hand-shaker." It is much more professional (and safe) to explain "negative-equity" and the advantages and disadvantages of a manual transmission.

Verbal communication is not a one-size-fits-all endeavor. Many factors (i.e., personalities, environment, circumstances, background, etc.) play a significant role in the flow and dynamics of a one-on-one or a group conversation. The same word, sentence, or story can be (and probably will be) interpreted in as many ways as there are people who hear the exact same word, the exact same sentence, or the exact same story.

Certain words, however, foster negative images and connotations. The word "no," as a general rule, is considered restrictive and non-negotiable. The words "yes" and "perhaps," also as a general rule, are widely viewed as less restrictive and in a less harsh manner. Both "yes" and "no" are the ultimate words in terms of commitment. In courts of law, lawyers are often opposed to asking their clients questions requiring a yes or no answer. Obviously, jurors (as well as the human psyche) have difficulties deciphering questions such as: "Do you still beat your wife?" When we think about it for a moment, how important is the lone word "still" in that particular inquiry?

The legacies of high-profile individuals are often set in stone from a single word or statement. President Franklin Roosevelt will forever be immortalized from his utterance: "We have nothing to fear – but fear itself." President John F. Kennedy will forever be revered for his charge: "Ask not, what your country can do for you; ask, what you can do for your country." President Richard Nixon etched an image in the minds of most Americans with his combative statement: "I am not a crook!" At the very moment he uttered "crook," Richard Nixon cemented his reputation as a "crook" into the history books and into the minds of his fellow citizens. President Bill Clinton will long be remembered for his dissection of the word "is."

Words have repercussions. We must use them carefully, selectively, and strategically. We can inspire and give confidence with our words, or we can deflate and instill apprehension.

I once worked with a gentleman who would gladly talk to a tree if there was no individual available. His name was Billy – and Billy loved conversation more than he loved air. Everyone who knew Billy was aware of his gift of gab — and dealt with it accordingly; total strangers, however, could be taken aback at a moment's notice. Billy loved people (and people loved Billy), and he was always the first person to arrive at work and the last person to leave. One day, Billy spotted a wayward pudgy person ambling across the showroom floor looking in need of direction (or idle conversation). The service customer was simply passing a few minutes while waiting for an oil-change. This customer was indeed a new person to the community and had recently taken a position as the nanny for a famous Christian singer in Nashville. Not to be deterred, Billy honed in on her like a heat-seeking missile, " Uh, ma'am, when's your baby due?" Shocked beyond belief, the lady (who was not pregnant) quickly responded, "I am not pregnant!" Needless to say, the showroom quickly resembled rats leaving a sinking ship as Billy retorted without a moment's hesitation, "Well, Thang said you wuz!" No one ever knew just who the hell "Thang" was; however, Billy adapted to the situation as best he could (using an escape-mechanism of posed senility). The mildly overweight lady was last seen looking dazed and confused as she shuffled back to the service waiting area. There is little doubt as to whether or not she ever visited the dealership again; she was obviously humiliated. Billy, on the other hand, never had another thought about the short-lived conversation. He simply went about his business of finding another individual with whom he could converse. Billy was (and is) a very nice elderly man: albeit, with no clue as to the ramifications of his words.

Adjectives can be an ally of professional sales professionals (and/or advertisers). In the 1970's, Ricardo Montalban was a leading Hollywood actor who starred in the popular *Fantasy Island* series. Montalban exuded an image of intelligence, sex-appeal, and exquisite taste.

In opportunistic fashion, Chrysler used an extensive long-term advertising campaign featuring Montalban swooning over a Chrysler Cordoba in exotic locales. He urged the buying public to sit on nothing but the "Corinthian leather" in the Cordoba. In reality, no one (not even Montalban) had a clue as to what the hell "Corinthian leather" was – or, what gave "Corinthian leather" a greater appeal than ordinary leather. The manner and accent in which "Corinthian leather" flowed from Montalban's tongue, however, clinched the ad campaign as a "classic" winner for Chrysler. It put legions of buyers in a mindset of buying a

Chrysler in order to get some "Corinthian leather." To this day, I'm not sure, but I suspect Ricardo Montalban moonlighted as a sex therapist.

Car shoppers all over America were asking for "Corinthian leather"; Mercedes-Benz dealers were fielding requests for "Corinthian leather." To say the least, "Corinthian leather" was a big hit – and no one even knew what it was! In fact, I'm still trying to determine what I want in my next car: "Corinthian leather" or "faux" leather!

William Shakespeare, one of history's foremost authorities on words, once said, "Words without thoughts never to heaven go." With his astute and thoughtful understanding of words, we should have little doubt that William Shakespeare and Ricardo Montalban shared a family tree. No doubt, William Shakespeare would have loved "Corinthian leather."

CHAPTER 5

COMMON GROUND...
A STEP TO SUCCESS

"For most women, the language of conversation is primarily a language of rapport: a way of establishing connections and negotiating relationships."
- Deborah Tannen

THE MOST CRITICAL seconds of a sales opportunity are the first thirty seconds. Knowing it is imperative to remove "the chill" from the encounter, a wise sales professional will use the entire thirty seconds (or longer if necessary) removing the angst from the consumer's psyche. During these initial seconds, most consumers are determining whether or not we fit their pre-determined stereotypical image of the infamous "car salesman." Many consumers would rather be hit in the head with a frying pan than interact with what they fully expect: a cigarette smoking, plaid-jacket wearing, back-slapping, pinky-ring adorning "car salesman" with retractable horns. When we initially introduce ourselves as "Darrell," all the consumer hears is "Devil." Obviously, it is of the utmost importance to turn that mindset around QUICKLY!

One of the best ways to successfully remove the false image is with a simple, enthusiastic and friendly "HELLO!" At this point, we are not in the "car business," we are in the "people business!" Our cars, trucks, and SUV's are totally insignificant until a reasonable comfort level (by both parties) is met. To my knowledge, no one has ever been offended by a sincere "hello." The standard car business line of "Can I help you?" is counter-productive to what we are seeking: open and free-flowing dialogue. It begs the response, "I'm just looking!" Instantly, of our own making, we put ourselves behind the eight ball and the consumer's defense mechanisms are on full alert; the consumer's angst level is increasing as opposed to what we really need: a decreasing level of angst. In this hypothetical situation, in a matter of seconds, the salesperson is hip-deep in troubles. It may be a hypothetical example, but it is all too common in today's automotive industry. Abraham Lincoln once said, "Better to remain silent and be thought a fool than to speak out and remove all doubt." Clearly, the sixteenth President of the United States never wore a plaid jacket or a pinky-ring with his top hat.

The wise salesperson initially engages his or her prospects with good-natured banter about the pretty day, the fresh air, last night's storm, tomorrow's high school football game, etc. It is critical to the ultimate outcome that we initially look for an opportunity to humanize ourselves away from the consumers' image of the "typical car salesman" so imprinted upon their mind. It also needs to be a stage for building a bridge to who they are in terms of where they live, where they work, where they went to school, how many kids they have, what hobbies and interests they enjoy, who their favorite team is, and/or anything that can provide common ground and foster rapport. Successfully finding connectors is an integral part of being productive in both volume and gross profits beyond the norm.

In baseball terms, it is highly unlikely for a salesperson to get to first base without finding connectors that subconsciously tell the consumer that he or she could share the same grocery store, dry cleaners, high school, club, subdivision, or place of worship with the salesperson. In other words, we have to be perceived as potentially his or her neighbor – and that it wouldn't be a bad thing!

I once worked with a gentleman salesperson who could spend two or three hours with a prospect and be oblivious to any details about where they resided, their profession, interests, spouse, children or any other pertinent information about what made this person in front of him tick. This salesperson was a prime example of the stereotypical "gear head"; he was, in his own eyes, employed in the "car business" as opposed to being employed in the "people business." He lectured to the prospect about every minute detail regarding specifications, automotive engineering, and competitive comparisons. In the end, the prospects frequently fled and the salesman continuously wondered why his income was abysmal and his production at the bottom of the sales chart. Having a vast array of product knowledge is great; however, it is virtually useless in and of itself. Product knowledge must be coupled with a thorough knowledge of the prospective buyer and his or her circumstances, needs, desires, and motivations.

We must constantly remind ourselves that automotive shoppers are looking for more than sheet metal and an emblem. Excellence in salesmanship, in my opinion, is nothing more than finding common ground with one's clientele to such an extent that the competition quietly falls by the wayside and is no longer a viable factor.

Sales representatives generally fall into one of three categories without regard to socio-economic conditions. The vast majority fall into the AVERAGE (and less than AVERAGE) category. These individuals fare poorly during recessions and times of economic upheaval. Their lack of structure, focus and/or a clear-cut GAME PLAN make them extremely vulnerable to less than sterling market conditions which often result in less floor traffic and a more cautious, deliberate, and value-conscious consumer.

Trackstar International, a follow-up and retention system corporation, estimates the "average" closing ratio in automotive sales at fifteen percent. Trackstar also estimates the "average" U.S. salesperson to have 55 floor traffic opportunities per month, resulting in 8.3 sales per month for the "average" salesperson. These numbers, it is important to note, fall within the range of commonly-held beliefs within the industry, with the numbers holding fairly steady throughout decades of automotive sales. A small amount of variation can be expected during periods of market turmoil such as 9/11 and the recession of 2008-2010. If these numbers are relatively close to correct, as most industry insiders believe, it rings an ominous note for the AVERAGE (and less than AVERAGE) salesperson who hopes to earn a decent living by doing the same unproductive routines and expecting fruitful results. We are all familiar with the oft-quoted definition of insanity: "doing the same thing over and over again and expecting different results."

In today's economic climate (tough!), "AVERAGE" salespersons (and "AVERAGE" dealerships), who do not change with the times (and learn from the past) are destined to extinction. Desperate times, it has been said, call for desperate measures. I disagree; desperate times call for a GAME PLAN!

Dealerships that employ "AVERAGE" salespersons – and fail to provide a structured format for improvement and achievement – are not only destined for possible extinction, but an ugly profit-loss statement in the interim. Dealerships that waste income opportunities by employing "AVERAGE" as opposed to "COMPETITIVE HIGH-ACHIEVER" salespersons squander the opportunity to enhance their bottom line by thousands (and in some cases tens of thousands) of dollars per month.

Most automobile dealerships employ one or more "ABOVE AVERAGE" salespersons. These individuals frequently have good people skills, know a fair amount about their products, and have decent closing and negotiating skills. They are, generally speaking, adaptable and persistent. The "ABOVE AVERAGE" salesperson is an asset to his or her organization; the "AVERAGE" salesperson is a liability.

During the course of an average month (or year), the "AVERAGE" salesperson is selling approximately one in six or seven of his or her opportunities. The "ABOVE AVERAGE" salesperson consistently produces at a one in five (or better) ratio. Little things mean a lot in the sales process; "ABOVE AVERAGE" sales professionals apply consistency and structure to their sales repertoire. As a general rule, "ABOVE AVERAGE" sales pros ask more pertinent questions and listen more intently than do "AVERAGE" salespersons. The pros, in simple terms, are probers!

Have you ever wondered why God formed Adam and Eve (and every Homo sapien since) with two ears and one mouth? Think about it for a minute! Why do ears enjoy a two-to-one ratio over mouths? Consumers provide valuable information about themselves when they speak – and we listen! The biggest step an "AVERAGE" salesperson can take toward "ABOVE AVERAGE" status is to listen more and speak less.

The third category of sales professionals is the COMPETITIVE ACHIEVER." These are the people Vince Lombardi would have loved! Lombardi once said, "If you can accept losing, you can't win." Professionals in the "COMPETITIVE ACHIEVER" category tend to be analytical and focused on the ultimate objective: winning! They hate losing more than they love winning; they win to avoid losing. As a general rule, "COMPETITIVE ACHIEVERS" also keep score.

It is a safe assumption that "COMPETITIVE ACHIEVERS" know (off the top of their heads) what their closing ratio is, how many units they have out for the month (and year), what their standing is for Salesman of the Month (and Salesman of the Year), and how many units are needed to meet their bonus and/or sales objective. These individuals are largely undeterred by market or economic conditions; they will simply find another route to their goal when an impediment exists. In hard times,

"COMPETITIVE ACHIEVERS" rise above the demoralized and the defeated. In some ways, "COMPETITIVE ACHIEVERS" are more dominant in difficult times. This is due in large part to an ever-increasing gap between high producers and low producers during adversity. During a tough market, "AVERAGE" salespersons make excuses and get weaker; "COMPETITIVE ACHIEVERS" get stronger.

Not all dealerships have a "COMPETITIVE ACHIEVER" and not all people have the capability to be one. Most often, a penchant for high achievement is somewhat innate; however, the traits can be learned and applied through sheer will and repetition – but only up to a certain point. Coach Lombardi also said, "Show me a good loser, and I'll show you a loser." Big-time producers are poor losers indeed. That is a trait which cannot be learned.

If the "AVERAGE" salesperson can simply learn to listen more intently, speak less, and paint a vivid picture of him or herself as the prospect's potential neighbor, production (both volume and gross profit) will begin to inch steadily away from "AVERAGE" status toward the more lucrative and stable "ABOVE AVERAGE" status. Improvement in Step Five (Finding Common Ground) of *SIXTEEN STEPS TO $IX-FIGURE$: A GAME PLAN FOR SALES SUCCESS* makes each proceeding step easier and more fluid. A successful Step Five begets a more successful Step Six. A successful Step Six begets a more successful Step Seven – and so on. You will be surprised and amazed how much smoother negotiations go when the prospect and the sales professional have a shared vision and/or memory of leisure activities, school activities, and community events. In sales, it is vital for us to know the same people our prospects know and to have experienced the same experiences they have experienced.

The close also becomes exponentially less stressful and part of a more natural flow when one's uncle worked with another's uncle for fifteen years. That is precisely the kind of information an "ABOVE AVERAGE" and "COMPETITIVE ACHIEVER" seek. Experienced sales pros know, for example, to look at the rear bumper of the prospect's trade-in. Stickers, bumper stickers, tags, and parking passes provide valuable insight into the life and values of a prospect.

In a nutshell, listen and learn; be perceptive and earn! There will be a time to move forward to the sheet metal; do not get the horse before the carriage and do not put the product or the price before the people.

CHAPTER 6

THE ASSUMPTIVE SALE...
A STEP TO SUCCESS

"Even if you are on the right track, you will get run over if you just sit there."

- Will Rogers

THERE IS AN old adage in the car business that says: "When two people meet – one person gets sold." Truer words have never been spoken; as a result, it would be of great benefit to anyone in sales to determine all the advantages and disadvantages associated with being the "sell-er" as opposed to being the "sell-ee."

We simply, as sales professionals, cannot afford to sit back and accept a "whatever happens - happens" result. To do so is paramount to "throwing in the towel;" we become the "sold" as opposed to being the "seller." To avoid being the "sold," we need to consistently take a proactive stance: getting out in front of the inevitable delays, excuses, smokescreens, and BS! Successful sales professionals anticipate objections and hurdles; they work toward developing an aura that makes several important nonverbal statements. Number one, my time is valuable; it is not acceptable for you or anyone else to waste my time (or your time). Number two, the environment in which we find ourselves is a place of business; why else would we find ourselves in this place, at this time, for any reason other than to "do business"? Number three, this is not Biltmore, the Grand Ole' Opry or the Grand Canyon; I am not a tour guide! In other words, successful sales professionals create an aura demanding respect; it is derived from building value in our product, building value in ourselves, building value in our place of business, and creating a true "sense of urgency" that results in a transaction beneficial to the consumer, the salesperson and the place of business. To do less is simply a disservice to all involved. Productive and successful sales people create a "sense of urgency" and ALWAYS assume the sale! What else is there to assume?

Experience tells us that most consumers repeatedly try to knock their sales consultant off his or her path or GAME PLAN. Why? It is an "out" for the consumer. It is a way in which the consumer can remain non-committal and safe; it is a way of "taking control" and becoming the "seller" instead of being the "sold." Unfortunately, in many respects, consumers are much better at this aspect of sales than most sales associates.

As sales professionals, we must never lose sight of these facts: number one, the consumer is our paycheck and not our enemy; without the consumer, there is no need for our services. Number two, the consumer deserves our respect (particularly for tenacity) as we too deserve his or her respect. Number three, our pride, our formulated talents, our competitive juices, and a GAME PLAN should equip us well against a formidable foe: the doggedly- determined consumer. Who should win these encounters? Most often, it will be the person (the consumer or the salesperson) "assuming the sale." In most instances, the leader will normally prevail over the led!

Early in my tenure as a Volvo sales representative, I spotted a disheveled man (with my periphery vision) one day entering the premises of the dealership on foot from an adjacent piece of property. Three salesmen in close proximity to the gentleman (obviously thinking he was a panhandler) quickly scattered in an attempt to avoid contact with him. At that point, the only barrier in front of me and the "panhandler" was the asphalt. Knowing all too well that the only thing worse than having to deal with a customer on foot was dealing with a customer on a bicycle (or motorcycle), I bit my lip and knew I had no choice but to take one for the team. Upon reaching the gentleman, I quickly learned he had serious car issues (it was broken beyond repair) and was mentally and emotionally ready for a new car and an end to his car hassles. I also learned (much to my surprise) the "panhandler" was a doctor (an anesthesiologist)!

As we began to walk through our inventory, I decided to eschew the typical qualifying process because I sensed that this was not an analytical buyer – instead, a highly emotional one. The twinkle in his eye was obvious as he peered at a glistening titanium Volvo S80 luxury sedan with upgrade wheels. I told him (not that he was listening to a word I said) that I would return in a minute with the key, and we would take it around the test loop. Upon returning, I opened the S80, removed it from its spot, walked him around the vehicle with a quick demonstration, and moved him into the driver's seat. I placed my knee on the pavement as I showed him the layout and the interior features; the look in his eyes was somewhat akin to a dog's gaze at their master while the master opens a new pack of rawhide bones.

As we took a right turn out of the dealership, he began to verbally express his favorable impression of the S80's ride quality. For once, I showed good judgment and kept quiet as he told me about himself, his family, his practice, his love for Volvo, and the recent frustrations he had encountered with his old jalopy. If ever there was a man ready for a new car – this was the man! During the test-drive, I came to the conclusion that nothing positive could come from my speaking; he was doing fine all by himself. I had never (and never since) built so much rapport by simply nodding.

Upon returning to the dealership, I noticed the three salesmen who had earlier scattered were looking at me as if I was "a few bricks shy of a load." I asked the doctor a question as we walked past them into the dealership: "Doctor, how do you want it to be titled?" The facial expressions of the three salesmen (with their mouths agape) was priceless!

The sale was a foregone conclusion as the doctor and I sat down. It was just a matter of how he wanted it titled, whether or not he wanted to finance or lease, and how to complete the necessary paperwork. There was nothing to negotiate; he wanted the car – and I wanted to sell it. The price was on the window. This was a sale that screamed for simplicity. "Doctor, please sign here," I said.

Within an hour of meeting the "panhandler," the doctor was riding home (without any hassles) in his new limousine (in his mind). The transaction was never cluttered with (or devalued by) terminology such as discounts, sale price, deal, etc.

The doctor was happy – and I was certainly happy. The transaction grossed $5,680.00 on the front end and $2,860.00 on the back end (finance rate, extended warranty, etc.). As a whole, the transaction grossed $8,540.00 and my commission was $1,563.00 – not bad for an hour's work dealing with a "panhandler."

I did not sell the doctor his Volvo S80; I simply let him buy it. Ironically, the doctor came back to see me three years later and traded.

He fought me like a wild cheetah for three hours – and I made next to nothing. As he left, I sat back in exhaustion and wondered what had happened between the first transaction and the second transaction. I came to the conclusion that his emotional motivation was not present when he traded; he simply made an analytical decision. I also came to the conclusion that analytical transactions may (at times) be necessary – but emotional ones are much more to my liking.

The "assumptive sale" does not work every time; in fact, it does not even work most of the time. It is, however, effective (and lucrative) some of the time.

One cannot afford, as a sales pro, to miss the infrequent occasions when the stars align and the "assumptive sale" falls into place and provides a quick, clean, fruitful, and enjoyable transaction for both the consumer and the sales professional. These transactions are so smooth and free of consternation that they consistently provide a bonus: perfect CSI (Customer Satisfaction Index) scores.

It is a wise sales professional who never strays far from "assumptive sale" mode.

CHAPTER 7

UNIQUENESS...
A STEP TO SUCCESS

"Today you are you, that is truer than true. There is no one alive who is youer than you."

- Dr. Seuss

"Do what others don't; don't what others do."

— Samuel Foust

THE BEST IS YOU

BELIEVE IN THE MORNING....
....AMID THE DAMPNESS OF DEW
BELIEVE IN THE EVENING....
....AS THE SUN SINKS ON CUE

BELIEVE IN ALWAYS....
....WITH NEVER IN VIEW
BELIEVE IN FOREVER....
....WHEN LIFE SEEMS THROUGH

BELIEVE IN THE OLD....
....CHERISH THE NEW
BELIEVE IN A LOVE....
....STRONG AND TRUE

BELIEVE IN GEMS AND CHANCES....
....AS RARE AND FEW
BUT MOST OF ALL...BELIEVE IN THE BEST
....FOR THE BEST IS YOU

----SAMUEL FOUST

IT HAS ALWAYS been my philosophy that attempting to be "better" is not always conducive to being "better." At times, it seems, being "different" is a much clearer path to attaining "better" status than simply working harder. It is quite possible that we are more productive and efficient when we "do what others don't – and don't what others do." Being "different" adds the element of "uniqueness" that is often missing from our day-to-day attempts to find success. If we aspire to being "better" than we were, "better" than the competition, or "better" than we previously thought we could be, using our "uniqueness" can be an important factor in raising the bar from where we were to higher levels to which we aspire.

First and foremost, it provides a major confidence boost when we realize we have innate and learned capabilities that other people do not possess. We all have DNA and experiences that can never be duplicated in another human being; even cloning cannot duplicate the person that we are, the person we have been, or the person that we will be in the future.

On the face of it, this perception may seem cocky, arrogant, and perhaps even narcissistic. Quite the contrary, our "uniqueness" can be utilized to benefit ourselves – and others – in a humble manner that recognizes that everyone else is "unique" as well. We certainly do not have an individual monopoly upon "uniqueness;" it is simply ours to use in a positive, negative, or neutral manner dependent upon how we choose to perceive and utilize it.

In reality, every person on earth is "unique;" every person who has ever lived is a totally "different" specimen than anyone else who has ever lived. We all have differing levels of abilities, talents, capabilities, and attributes. What we choose to do with our "uniqueness" is a personal decision based upon beliefs, values, backgrounds, goals, personalities, and a host of motivating factors. Some people choose to accentuate their "uniqueness" with flair; other people choose less colorful ways in which to separate themselves from the masses. Every person has a "unique" manner in which he or she relates to (or manages) his or her "uniqueness."

The late film producer and Disney founder Walt Disney once said, "The more you like yourself, the less you are like anyone else, which makes you unique." It is important to note that Walt Disney may have been the twentieth century's foremost expert on "uniqueness." He coupled his own "uniqueness" with a vivid imagination to give the world a gift of the iconic figure synonymous with "uniqueness:" Mickey Mouse!

For our business interests, it is important to realize that large segments of the general public are drawn to people, places, products, ideas, businesses, personalities, and concepts that are perceived as "unique:" the "norm" and the "status quo" are considered less desirable. The "unique" people, places, products, ideas, businesses, personalities, and concepts are often considered to be less boring and more exciting; substance (good, bad, or indifferent) frequently takes a back seat to the "uniqueness" variable. As a result, the people, places, products, ideas, businesses, personalities, and concepts accentuating their "uniqueness" quotient are widely considered to be more marketable and find themselves in greater demand than are their counterparts that are viewed as "less unique." In short, people, places, products, ideas, businesses, personalities, concepts, (and sales professionals) are often rewarded opportunities by the general public when the "uniqueness" quotient is fully accentuated.

Dennis Rodman may have been a good NBA defender and Boy George may possess melodic skills; it is a safe assumption, however, that each acquired the bulk of their fame and fortune from the "uniqueness" quotient. Either could be the modern-day poster boy for eighteenth century Swiss philosopher and essayist Jean Jacques Rousseau's self-analysis, "I may not be better than other people, but at least I'm different."

Living our daily lives and conducting our sales career in a manner aping what we see (and who we see) is a recipe to minimize (and to not take full advantage of) our "uniqueness" and to blend in with the crowd. Dr. Seuss, famous for his plethora of children's books, once offered sage advice, "Be who you are and say what you feel because those who mind don't matter and those who matter don't mind."

It is a tragedy, in my opinion, when we shield our "uniqueness" from the view of others. Our "uniqueness" is the largest component of who we are; it is the very essence of our being. Our "uniqueness" affords us the opportunity to see what others have not seen, to think what others have not thought, to feel emotions others have not felt, to achieve what others have not achieved, and to invent, process, and develop that which has never been invented, processed, or developed.

As a result, we have an obligation to ourselves, our employers, our clientele, our society, and to the "greater-good" to utilize our "uniqueness" in a manner that is wide open with possibilities.

French couturier Cocco Chanel once observed, "In order to be irreplaceable one must always be different." It is a wise and valued man or woman who presents the "irreplaceable" aura to his or her family, friends, employer, clientele, and community.

We are "unique" one and all; we are as "special" as any president; we are as "different" as any king. Author Michel de Montaigne once mused, "Even on the highest throne in the world, we are still setting on our ass." Let us never lose sight, as we sit on our throne of "uniqueness," that we are not sitting on just any ordinary ass; we are sitting on our very own "unique" ass.

CHAPTER 8

VALUE...
A STEP TO SUCCESS

"What we obtain too cheap, we esteem too lightly; it is dearness only that gives everything its value."
                                                    - Thomas Paine

IF, AS THOMAS Paine once suggested, "value" is intrinsically tied to "dearness," the products we sell and the ideas we espouse are of little value to the masses unless there is an aura of rarity and exclusivity, and a perception of demand exceeding supply. French Emperor Napoleon Bonaparte once noted, "There are two levers to set a man in motion, fear and self-interest." Successful sales professionals innately realize (or learn through trial and error) that nothing builds value quite like a "fear of loss" or the "self-interest" aspect of a product, service or opportunity that is perceived to be available only in small quantities to a select group of individuals during a narrow window of opportunity.

It is commonly believed that people, want what they cannot have. A millionaire wants to be a billionaire; a billionaire wants to be a multibillionaire. Every man wants the "girl who got away," and every woman wants the "man of her dreams." The toddler wants the toy in the next crib. The Bentley owner aspires to a Rolls-Royce and the Rolls-Royce owner aspires to a Bentley. Whatever falls outside our grasp is innately deemed to be of greater value than that which is within our grasp; it is often referred to as human nature.

Even in the animal kingdom, the angst of "what could have been" and the basic instinct to want what is "off-limits" is common. A dog in a dog pen, for example, wants his bone; however, he wants the bone in the adjacent dog pen even more than the bone dangling from his mouth. It is a wise and seasoned sales professional who realizes (and plans accordingly) that whatever we are selling is more desirable when it is rare, fleeting, limited, exclusive, off-limits, unavailable, or better yet, taken by someone else. Mignon McLaughlin, writer of *The Second Neurotics Notebook* once penned, "Anything you lose automatically doubles in value."

Value is a term that many use; yet, it is fully understood by few. Value is comprised of two forms; one being real – yet, fluctuating. The second form is imaginary – and open to conditions, perceptions, and emotions.

We all know the "value" of a dollar may equal seven krona today – but only worth six krona next week due to fluctuations in currency values. That "value" (real – yet, fluctuating) is largely insignificant to the typical consumer and salesperson relationship unless it has some bearing on our objectives ("urgency") or a consumer's fear (i.e., fear of loss, fear of mounting cost factors, etc.). On occasions the two forms of values can overlap and provide ideal closing opportunities for the astute sales professional who has the mindset to capitalize upon the aura of urgency prevalent within oscillating markets.

What is typically paramount to the sales process is the "imaginary" value that is relayed to and fro through emotions (i.e., fear of loss), perceptions (i.e., rare and exclusive), and conditions (i.e., demand exceeding supply). Hsi-Tang Chih Tsang, Zen master during the eighth century, understood value at its very core when he stated, "Although gold dust is precious, when it gets in your eyes it obstructs your vision." Clearly, understanding the complexities and nuances surrounding the concept of "value" is as vital today as it was hundreds of years ago when His-Tang Chih Tsang so eloquently placed the "preciousness" of gold dust in perspective, and Thomas Paine gave us a glimpse of the "dearness" element often missing in our assessment of "value."

So, how do we best "build value" in today's ultra-competitive business climate? First and foremost, we must exhibit a respect and admiration for our product, service, or idea. We must place our "valued commodity" on a higher plane than that which is average, typical, and/or easily attainable.

The antithesis of "value" is heard in ads, banners, promotional material, and general conversation on a regular basis. It often seems as if advertisers and sales associates cannot sell or advertise without "devaluing" their products with constant references to "deals," "sales," "discounts," and a host of red-flag terminology. Automobile dealers and sales professionals who aspire to a professional sales process that emphasizes "value" should strike those three words (deals, sales, discounts) from their lexicon; they are the very antithesis of "value." How can we, as sales professionals, build the confidence of our clientele when we are telling them (through our actions and language) the market for our product is somewhat akin to a "FIRE SALE!?" In the real world, extreme "hype" places a chilling effect on the consumer's propensity to "pull the trigger." We should never forget that people want what is difficult or impossible to obtain. What is easily obtained is much less desirable – and pays much less profit in the event we are able to salvage an "ugly" deal.

When lot attendants place thirty Honda Accords on the front-row, how is it possible for the consumer to feel a sense of urgency? Will they all be gone tomorrow? This common practice makes a huge statement to the consumer ("They're a dime a dozen!"). This practice is a classic example of supply and demand in reverse (as it relates to urgency); three or four on the front row would not only suffice – it would paint a more positive image regarding the status of our product. We would be well served to always remember the old English Proverb that says, "We never know the worth of water 'til the well is dry."

If we do not know the "worth" of our product, it would behoove us to assume its "worth" at a very high level. To elevate one's product to elite status by placing it on a (so-called) pedestal provides an "edge" in the sales process that many salespersons never (or rarely) pursue. Nineteenth-century poet, Oscar Wilde, once stated, "Nowadays people know the price of everything and the value of nothing." We would also be well served as sales professionals to de-emphasize "price" and emphasize the positive aspects of our products, services, and ideas that make them rare, unique, special, finite, fleeting, peerless, incomparable, and most importantly, one-of-a-kind!

Charles Dudley Warner, a nineteenth-century American writer, once wrote, "There is no such thing as absolute value in this world. You can only estimate what a thing is worth to you." If the late Mr. Warner was correct, today's professional salesperson would be much more productive and perceived by his or her clientele in a much more positive light by exhibiting the highest level of "value" for his or her product. Consumers are not a microcosm of society; they are society. Society has always "valued" products, services, people, and ideas that are highly esteemed;

when we as professional salespersons hold our products in high regard - our clientele follow suit.

Those of us who have worked for years within the retail automotive industry can recall many occasions when vehicles became old and tired within the inventory. Everyone became doubtful as to whether or not that particular vehicle would ever sell (at any price); it was the lone exception to the old adage, "there's an ass for every seat." In the end, however, not only did the vehicle sell, it sold to one "lucky" buyer who was fighting over it in the parking lot with an "unlucky" prospect who came in an hour late and a dollar short. In their minds, both consumers knew they were looking at a "unique" vehicle (or opportunity) too good to be true and desired by every consumer within a seventy-five mile radius. We would be wise to never forget the importance of never underestimating the "in their minds" component of the consumer psyche. Productive and efficient sales personnel realize that our perceptions and consumer perceptions are rarely one and the same.

Five thousand people can walk past an "ugly-duckling" product and perceive little (if any) value; when the five-thousand and first person begins to gaze amorously at the stance of this glorious piece of machinery, it is common for the five-thousand and second person (seeing the five-thousand and first person seizing an opportunity) to hyperventilate on the spot.

Beauty, it has often been said, is in the "eye of the beholder." Let us never forget an equally true aspect of human nature: value is in the "mind of the denied."

CHAPTER 9

PLAN...
A STEP TO SUCCESS

"Good fortune is what happens when opportunity meets with planning."

- Thomas Edison

"By failing to prepare, you are preparing to fail."
- Benjamin Franklin

IT IS QUITE possible to fail while having a "plan" for success. However, the odds of success are much greater when following a "plan," as opposed to taking a "by-the-seat-of-the-pants" approach. Even though there are no guarantees of victory with a "game plan," few coaches would send their team out for competition without first implementing a "plan" which would accentuate the strengths of his or her team and focus upon exploiting the weaknesses of the opponent. In our sales career, if we pursue great and lofty endeavors, we would be well served to remember the old proverb, "He who fails to plan, plans to fail."

When we admiringly watch a competitive team win a Super Bowl, World Series, Final Four, or Olympic gold medal, it most likely is the result of much more than luck or chance. It is safe to assume that Tiger Woods did not win numerous "Majors," nor did Lance Armstrong win the Tour de France on multiple occasions without first constructing "plans" which focused on best-case scenarios, worst-case scenarios, and possible factors beyond their control (i.e., weather, illnesses, schedules, etc.).

Legendary University of Alabama football coach Paul "Bear" Bryant once said, "Have a plan. Follow the plan, and you'll be surprised how successful you can be. Most people don't have a plan. That's why it's easy to beat most folks."

Creating a detailed "plan" provides structure and a framework by which one can move steadily and consistently from the beginning of an endeavor to its conclusion. It tells us what we intend to achieve, how we intend to achieve it, and when our objective will be completed. A well-constructed "plan" often proves to be the catalyst for direction, focus, motivation, organization, and confidence. Conversely, not having a "plan" is a recipe for havoc, disorganization, misdirection, a loss of control, and the inability to overcome the unexpected. In other words, we put our ultimate fate (as it relates to success or failure) in the hands of others, and place our objective in jeopardy when we are deficient in planning.

Norman Vincent Peale, author of *THE POWER OF POSITIVE THINKING*, once advised, "Plan your work – work your plan." When we formulate solid "plans," we have the potential to pursue relentlessly; when we fail to have solid "plans," we have the possibility of being relentlessly pursued by failure. In the competitive world of professional sales, who is more likely to find and achieve success – the predator or the prey?

Many people erroneously believe there is little difference between goal setting and planning. Nothing could be farther from the truth; goal setting is only a part (albeit, an important part) of a well-structured "plan." If one only has a goal, he or she has only a portion of a "plan." A solid and well-structured "plan" should include the following:

1. a tangible and measurable goal
2. a time frame to reach steps within the stated goals or objective
3. a time frame to reach the ultimate goal or objective
4. a written analysis and statement of resources needed to achieve the stated goal and how the resources will be allocated and utilized
5. an analysis of potential obstacles and how they can be minimized, overcome, and/or negated
6. an assessment of ways to accentuate strengths and minimize weaknesses in relation to executing the steps necessary to achieve the stated goal
7. an analysis and thorough understanding of the competition (their tendencies, their strengths, their weaknesses) and what must be done to defeat the competition
8. an alternative plan anticipating the worst-case scenario and /or the competition being stronger and more viable than anticipated

Professional boxer Mike Tyson once said, "Everyone has a plan – until they get punched in the face." As professional salespersons, we should anticipate our plan will not be completed without adversity and unexpected barriers. It would be naïve and risky to believe our "plan" can be carried out entirely as planned. He who expects the unexpected will be better positioned to deal with the inevitable bumps along the way. British Prime Minister Winston Churchill once said, "Those who plan do better than those who do not plan even though they rarely stick to their plan."

It has often been said, "The car business is a numbers game." If that is true (and I believe it is), then it would be in our own self-interest to focus upon how we can link our "plan" to the numbers necessary to reach our goals and objectives. Is our real world closing ratio conducive to meeting or exceeding our goals? Are we placing ourselves in front of enough qualified prospects to make the production-equation (O "opportunities" X CR "closing-ratio" = P "production") balance with our ultimate objective? In simple terms, for optimum results, our "plan" must be in balance with our objective in much the same manner as an accountant's credits and debits.

Over 1,600 years ago, Chinese General Sun Tzu stated, "Plan for what is difficult while it is easy, do what is great while it is small. The difficult things in the world must be done while they are easy; the greatest things in the world must be done while they are still small. For this reason Sages never do what is great, and this is why they achieve greatness."

In professional sales, if we devise a large plan with small parts, we have an opportunity to achieve our objective. Since there are no guarantees of success (with or without a plan), sales professionals would be wise to familiarize themselves with the methodology of a man who made the most of his opportunities; Thomas Edison, holder of 1,093 patents (the most in recorded history), always worked with a "plan." To achieve success, having a "plan" is not enough; we must execute the "plan" with patience, diligence, and a remembrance of Paul "Bear" Bryant's wise words about the consequences of not having a plan.

CHAPTER 10

NEGOTIATING SKILLS...
A STEP TO SUCCESS

"If you can't go around it, over it, or through it, you had better negotiate with it."

- Chester C. Karrass

IN THE RETAIL automotive industry, the best negotiations are no negotiations at all. How could that be? Well, in the perfect world, all consumers would make the professional salesperson's job "a piece of cake;" the "assumptive sale" would work each and every time, and we would all live and work in Utopian environments. In the real world, where the professional salesperson's job is not "a piece of cake," most transactions must be brought to fruition via negotiations.

In automotive transactions, consumers and sales associates desire diametrically opposed results. The consumer wants to pay "the least possible;" the salesperson wants the consumer to pay "the most possible." Quite often, consumers feel as if there is a "best-deal number" the salesperson is concealing; salespersons feel frustrated by consumers who believe there is "a magical number" that can be pulled out of a hat, and then want to make a counter offer after they have acquired what they asked for: "the best-deal number." As sales professionals, how do we meander diplomatically through such a convoluted sales environment with our sanity and "plan" intact?

An old saying states, "You must be fully prepared to lose a great deal in order to make a great deal." As the seller, when we negotiate with a "fear of loss" mentality, strength and dominance is transferred from the seller to the buyer; therefore, completing an agreement becomes exponentially more difficult (if not impossible) and profitability is compromised. When we negotiate with an "aura of strength and confidence," the consumer instinctively becomes more flexible and open to our suggestions and proposals; consequently, the transaction becomes more fluid and profitable. A topnotch salesperson, negotiating with an "aura of strength and confidence" can often create a "seller's market" when he or she is actually in the midst of a "buyer's market!"

The key to successful negotiations can be found in the work leading up to negotiations. If dialogue is difficult or at an impasse, it is quite likely steps have been missed or diluted during the sales process. Has rapport and common ground been established? Has the client been qualified to the extent his or her needs, wants, and budget limitations have been ascertained? Is the ultimate decision maker present?

In short, it is extremely difficult to "fit a square peg through a round hole." As sales professionals, it is important to make sure every step leading up to negotiations is in alignment with our ultimate objective: a closed and profitable sale!

It is imperative to obtain some semblance of a commitment from a client before beginning negotiations; such a commitment can be a simple verbal acknowledgement of intent to do business "sooner rather than later" if terms and conditions are acceptable. It is quite important to obtain and retain "eye contact" when "intent" is disclosed. Prussian statesman Otto Von Bismarck once correctly stated, "When a man says that he approves something in principle, it means he hasn't the slightest intentions of putting it in practice." In other words, get commitments in writing (when possible), and always beware of the consumer who states he or she "doesn't want to haggle;" for he or she is the very consumer who will "haggle" until the "cows come home." The "I don't want to haggle" consumer is simply attempting to back his or her salesperson into a corner before negotiations ever take place. If we comply with the "no haggle" consumer's wishes, the consumer will "begin negotiations" once we have "ended negotiations." This predicament is commonly referred to as an "impasse." Most assuredly, the "no haggle" prospect is unwittingly telling us that he or she has no intention of negotiating "in good faith."

Failure to obtain a commitment often results in providing "outs" for the client during negotiations. In the real world, consumers are not engaging in negotiations (in their mind, they are only discussing) until a verbal and/ or signed commitment is made. Every business person, without regard to specificity of industry, would be well served by the realization the most fruitless endeavor (and a waste of time) is an attempt at negotiating when only one side is negotiating! The most critical element of negotiations is obtaining a commitment from one's counterpart; nothing is achievable in negotiations until a commitment is extracted from one's fellow negotiator.

During negotiations, the initial proposal should be presented by the "seller." It has often been said that when one finds him or herself in a fistfight, it is advisable to "land the first punch." In negotiations, to do otherwise provides a perceived "window of opportunity" whereby the "buyer" offers a "low-ball" scenario; the "seller" being at a great disadvantage when having to climb upward to reach an agreement – as opposed to moving downward in small increments. From the "seller's" vantage point, it is more productive (and ultimately more profitable) to be moving downward from fifteen thousand dollars – as opposed to moving upward from ten thousand dollars.

In professional negotiations, it is advisable to avoid the devastating consequences of a "deal-killing" and "profit-killing" gap between two parties; an objective most easily accomplished when the "seller" fires the "initial salvo" and presents acceptable terms, conditions, and prices before the "buyer" offers an unacceptable and unrealistic proposal. In the real world, when given the opportunity, it is not uncommon for a consumer to demand a $300.00 monthly payment when considering a $30,000.00 car. The math simply doesn't work – a fact that the consumer fully realizes. It is a tactic designed to intimidate and manipulate. As a result, in this scenario, it would not be a bad idea to immediately (and unapologetically) request the necessary $20,000.00 down payment.

Once a proposal has been presented to a client, one's next move can be summed up in one word: SILENCE! The old adage, "He who speaks first –loses," should be incorporated into the basic strategy of every negotiator. We should never get in the way of a fellow negotiator's opportunity to say "yes" or "no." Obviously, a "yes" is the ideal scenario; however, a "no" can be dealt with easily as well. A "yes" should be immediately acted upon in terms of the steps (or paperwork) needed to "seal the deal." A "no" should be immediately acted upon in terms of finding the obstacle standing in the way of an agreement. It is important to realize a "no" is simply a "yes" in need of tweaking or a minor adjustment. DO NOT overreact to a "no;" it can actually be construed as a good thing (a "buying sign"). The only mindset for a negotiator to possess is: a "no" is a "yes" in the making.

Once negotiations begin, the atmosphere needs to be "all business." Otherwise, distractions creep into the process and create a loss of momentum, a loss of focus, and/or a loss of urgency; all three being critical elements of successful negotiations.

In a perfect scenario, the flow of negotiations remains constant and consistent. The strategic use of time is vital to achieving two major objectives: getting the agreement sealed and getting the agreement sealed in a profitable manner. The old car business adage, "Eighty percent on your feet – and twenty percent on your seat," is accurate in terms of the most productive selling and closing ratio. For example, eighty minutes spent building rapport, building value, creating urgency, and overcoming objections should immediately be followed by a maximum of twenty minutes in negotiations to reach a mutual agreement. Closing ratios and levels of profitability begin to drop dramatically once the 80/20 ratio moves to a 79/21 (and narrowing) ratio. Once the 80/20 ratio is breached, most of the "giving" comes from the "seller;" at that point, the prospective "buyer" senses "blood in the water" and may often express the need to "sleep on it." As all experienced sales professionals know, stalled and slow-moving negotiations are disastrous for closing ratios.

The most important trait of a successful negotiator is his or her ability to create a perception for the fellow negotiator that "the last dime has been squeezed" from the agreement. No one wants to feel as if he or she has "left money on the table." A good negotiator takes the time to delve into the psyche of his or her counterpart; knowing the attitude, tendencies, and motivations of one's competition is essential in determining the hows, whys, and whens of strategy.

He who negotiates without speed, strategy, and structure – negotiates poorly. In today's economic climate, ineffective negotiating skills are a ticket to the unemployment line or the soup line. German statesman Konrad Adenauer once stated, "The one sure way to conciliate a tiger is to allow oneself to be devoured." As sales professionals, we need not "devour" our negotiating adversaries, but we should never fail to underestimate our counterparts who may or may not want to "devour" us!

A straightforward approach to fruitful negotiations, in my opinion, is similar to the basic formula needed for a successful sex life: neither party needs to get screwed more (nor less) than the other; both parties will, ideally, participate; and in a perfect world, both participants will finish at the same time! Just a word of caution - since I have never participated in threesomes (or multiple party) negotiations, my advice only applies to one-on-one negotiations!

CHAPTER 11

ADAPTABILITY...
A STEP TO SUCCESS

"One learns to itch where one can scratch."

- Ernest Braman

RANKING RIGHT ALONG with good people skills and the ability to create urgency, the most common attribute of high-achieving sales professionals is: adaptability. Most (if not all) quality salespersons can "think on their feet" and take a potentially negative or neutral situation and produce a more positive or forward-moving situation by executing a step or a series of steps thought up "on the fly." If one step (or remedy) does not work, the "adaptable" salesperson simply moves on to another step (or remedy) that does. High-achieving individuals often believe in the old adage: "Hills are no problem for a climber."

Abraham Maslow, widely known as the father of humanistic psychology, once stated, "To the man who only has a hammer, everything he encounters begins to look like a nail." An experienced sales professional comes to realize through both success and failure that sometimes a "nail" must be hammered with whatever is available when a hammer is nowhere to be found. Therefore, he or she tends to collect a wider array of tools (resources, strategies, alternatives, etc.) to use when it becomes clear that "nails" come in a variety of sizes, shapes, and forms. In the real world, "nails" often refuse to cooperate with a "hammer."

Having alternatives potentially counters the mass and dynamics that dominate the space between the "less than ideal" situation where we often find ourselves and a space more conducive to our advantage. Former Israeli Prime Minister Shimon Peres once stated, "When you have two alternatives, the first thing you have to do is to look for the third that you didn't think about, that doesn't exist." In short, when we limit our options, we also limit our possibilities. It is difficult to be "adaptable" when we look at a situation from a sole perspective or have only one path leading to our goals and objectives.

In the automotive industry, we are frequently confronted by people and bombarded by situations that drag negativity to our doorsteps. A salesperson who has the "adaptability" necessary to transform negatives into positives and tense situations into calm ones is an asset to a corporation that permeates throughout the sales environment all the way to the bottom line. If we ever take on the task of finding the truly indispensable person within an organization, the search will begin and end with the most "adaptable" employee.

The polar opposite of "adaptability" is "rigidity." When we are "rigid" and void of creativity and innovativeness, negatives are often barriers that we cannot overcome; a potential positive is never pursued because it will be perceived as "too difficult" or onerous to achieve. Total "rigidity" in a sales environment is a classic example of defeatism. "Rigidity" dictates it can't happen, it won't happen, it shouldn't happen, it couldn't happen, it hasn't happened before, and it mustn't happen because no one knows what would happen if it happened! "Adaptability," on the other hand, suggests it can happen, it will happen, it should happen, it could happen, and it must happen because "good things" will most assuredly happen if it happens. The fact that it hasn't happened before, to the "adaptable" one, only indicates that whatever it is that needs to happen, it is long overdue; the right methodology has not been applied and a winning strategy has not been formulated. Wise sales professionals who exhibit "adaptability" see a "no!" as a puzzle needing to be solved into a "yes!" They also see "negatives" as "hills in need of being climbed," with "positives" to be found at the summit. Whenever he or she does a product demonstration to a prospect, the truly "adaptable" sales professional cannot wait to show the drag coefficient forward of the B-pillar at the apex of the "unique" vehicle on display. The "rigid" sales person (who never looks or explores beyond the surface) doesn't know an apex from a duplex!

"Adaptability" is a mindset; it is a belief that what "is" does not necessarily have to be a permanent state. In essence, "adaptable" people are first and foremost "problem-solvers." Just as a massive pile-up on the interstate requires an assessment of the situation at hand, an exit ramp, and alternative routes to a predetermined destination, daily obstacles require an analytical approach to avoid being sidetracked when "things don't go as planned." "Problem solvers" are fully cognizant of the predetermined destination; the route can and will change, however, when the necessity arises or when a better route becomes available.

Spiro T. Agnew, former United States Senator and Vice President, once stated, "In the United States today, we have more than our share of the nattering nabobs of negativism." "Adaptable" sales professionals are, as a general rule, the antithesis of "the nattering nabobs of negativism." They are largely immune to stimuli not conducive to their goals and objectives; they have the ability to find good in the midst of bad, sanity in the midst of chaos, optimism in the midst of negativism, reason in the midst of the unreasonable, success in the midst of the unsuccessful, and enthusiasm in the midst of the unenthused.

He who practices "adaptability" does not abandon his principles in the company of the unprincipled; she who practices "adaptability" does not abandon her ethics in the company of the unethical. The "adaptable" one embraces his or her own high standards and flourishes – in the company of one and all – one way or another!

CHAPTER 12

BELIEVABILITY...
A STEP TO SUCCESS

"An open ear is the only believable sign of an open heart."

- David Augsburger

WALTER CRONKITE HAD "it," and "it" was the most important element of his widespread reputation as "the most trusted man in America." President Lyndon Johnson, during the height of the Vietnam War, once lamented, "If I've lost Cronkite, I've lost Middle America." What did "Uncle Walter" (as he was affectionately known by the American people) possess that elevated him to the extraordinary perch he enjoyed in the psyche of the American public? Walter Cronkite did, unquestionably, on a more profound level, what no other public figure in American culture has done since George ("I cannot tell a lie.") Washington; he exuded "believability" from every fiber of his being! As a result, "Uncle Walter" enjoyed a status and public persona during his professional career that negated his competition for the airways to non-factor status. How can sales professionals, albeit in a different era, have just a little of what Walter Cronkite had in abundance? The more important question is: How can sales professionals, in competitive and ultra-competitive sales environments, defeat and dominate their competition into non-factor status?

In the opening chapter of *SIXTEEN STEPS TO $IX-FIGURE$: A GAME PLAN FOR SALES SUCCESS*, a major emphasis is placed upon building each sales opportunity and our career in much the same manner as one builds a house. Since we must first build a foundation (an understanding of failure as it relates to success), before we install a roof (believability), we must successfully integrate all the processes between the foundation and the roof. In essence, Walter Cronkite built his house (journalism and broadcasting) in an orderly and sequential manner. His believability (his roof) was a by-product of all the work he did before getting in front of the camera. His on-air deliveries were natural (and believable), and the culmination of days, weeks, and often years of work, experience, and knowledge. Walter Cronkite earned the right to say, "And that's the way it is." He also earned his reputation (believable) by being thorough, consistent, and doing due diligence before relaying information to the American people. As a result, he "believed" the accuracy of that which he spoke. Without a doubt, Walter Cronkite knew achieving "believability" was highly unlikely without a backdrop for its display, for we cannot attain believability until we first believe. We should never forget that a roof without a foundation is impossible and a house without a roof is a disaster!

Edward R. Murrow, another renowned communicator of yore, once mused, "To be persuasive we must be believable; to be believable we must be credible; credible we must be truthful."

It is obvious that both Walter Cronkite and Edward R. Murrow understood the correlation and link between truthfulness and credibility, credibility and believability, and believability and persuasiveness – all crucial elements in professional endeavors from broadcasting to politics to salesmanship.

It is often said that professional sales representatives should, to maximize effectiveness, build credibility with their clientele. It is rare that anyone ever speaks as to how that objective can best be accomplished.

Credibility does not "just happen." It is a by-product and an end result of everything that transpires before one can be accurately labeled as "believable." Being "believable," in the sales arena, is a constant work-in-progress that requires self-analysis of one's image and perceived knowledge encased in forthrightness and espoused in an emphatic tone. Our verbal skills must also align in direct proportion with our nonverbal signals to those in our presence if our verbal output is to be believed.

Just as a well-known equation (a positive and a negative equals a negative) suggests, a direct and "believable" oratory married to a fidgety and eye-contact-avoiding physical presence is a red flag when communicating which can be difficult to overcome if one wishes to be "believable" and credible.

We derive far better results when we couple a positive with a positive. This equation also increases the likelihood of our ultimate success when people form an opinion as to whether or not they wish to deal with us on a personal and/or professional basis. Otherwise, and much to our chagrin, we may simply be labeled as "a nattering nabob of negativism."

CHAPTER 13

NICHES…
A STEP TO SUCCESS

"We live in a niche world."

- Leigh Steinberg

T MAY SOUND like an old cliché; however, in today's ultra-competitive automotive industry, doing (and finding) the "little things" is unquestionably the difference between success and failure. Many years ago, I worked with an above-average salesman named Kurt who was selling Toyota Camrys like hotcakes. It was early in my tenure at that dealership, and Kurt had been selling more Camrys than the rest of the dealership's sales personnel combined. Needless to say, my curiosity was piqued (big time), and I just had to know what he was doing or saying to make people stand in line to buy Camrys from him. On top of his extraordinary levels of volume, his transactions seemingly flowed well with minimal amounts of negotiations. To say the least, Kurt's customers were not playing hardball or being obstinate or noncommittal at the negotiating table. In overwhelming numbers, they were taking his first proposal and not even making counteroffers. From my vantage point, it seemed as if he was not only selling voluminous amounts of Camrys – but he was also making high levels of gross profits (and commissions) as well.

One morning, I decided to ask Kurt what his secret was. "So, Kurt, let me ask you something," I said. "What are you doing or saying to sell all these Camrys day after day with so much success?" "Well, Sam," he said, "I just take all the middle-aged to older men back to the trunk and open it. Just when they expect me to start telling them about cargo space and what not, I pull the floor up and show them the real spare tire as I tell them the Camry is the only car in its class that doesn't use that cheap ol' temp tire. Sam, the older men stand there with a grin on their face, and it looks like they're going to have an orgasm! From that point on, it's like taking candy from a baby."

At that moment, I knew Kurt was on to something and had found a "little thing" and made a very "big thing" out of it. In reality, he had found one of the Camry's "niches" and exploited it to his advantage versus the remainder of the competition. Without question, Kurt deserved an A+ in Salesmanship 101.

By finding (and displaying) his product's "niche," he covered a lot of ground in the areas of value, desirability, and utilizing the law of supply and demand by simply going for the jugular with a spare tire. Those of us in sales (any area of sales) should stop and think about Kurt's effective strategy. He used a fifty dollar tire to sell a twenty thousand dollar vehicle. It puts to rest any doubt about whether or not sales productivity is largely attributable to doing "the little things" such as finding a "niche" to one's advantage.

Kurt did not need to bash his competition. His customer's visual image of a real spare tire, coupled with the reinforcement of a low-key verbal shot at "that cheap ol' temp tire" often placed a mental image (and possibly even a subliminal message) in the minds of his customers that elevated the Camry's desirability quotient above that of its rivals. Without saying it verbally, Kurt's subtle prod basically injected a doubt about the "quality" of the competition into the minds of his customers. After all, if a manufacturer will place "that cheap ol' temp tire" in the trunk, what (pray tell) will they do under the hood? When those doubts crept in, it wasn't long before Kurt's customers began peering at the quality (or flaws) of the fabric and/or dash materials of the competition as well. Kurt did what he had the opportunity to do; he devalued his competition with a spare tire that he (and he alone) possessed.

Quite likely, had the Camry not possessed a real spare tire, Kurt would simply have found another relevant "niche" to exploit. It could have been anything from the gauge of the sheet metal (versus the Honda Accord) to a host of other possibilities. Quite often, Kurt sold his prospects on their first visit to the dealership. A high percentage of those who did not "hook-up" on their initial visit, returned to purchase from Kurt after taking a wary look at his rivals. It is a safe assumption that when the consumer shopped, the consumer found very few (if any) sales associates finding and/or displaying his or her product's "niche" to the level Kurt found and displayed his. It is also a safe assumption that Kurt's customers, when shopping the Camry versus the competition, always made a beeline to the trunk to check out the status of the spare. It is another safe assumption that I would not have wanted to be the competitive salesperson when the prospect opened up the floor of the trunk after Kurt's earlier presentation of the Camry.

To put Kurt's strategy into perspective, we must stop and think about how effective (and profitable) his one "niche" was in the entire process of selling a vehicle in an ultra-competitive market. It simply engulfed both the car-buying and the car-selling processes. That is not to say that Kurt did a poor job in the other critical areas of salesmanship (meeting and greeting, qualifying, finding common ground, etc.); it does point out, however, that his foray into finding his product's "niche" (a rarity in the sales process) gave him a little breathing room from which he could recover if he was not at the top of his game in one or more of those areas. In fact, if his competition was equal to the task in all the other important aspects of the sales process, Kurt most likely was the winner by virtue of the tiebreaker (finding his product's "niche")!

Kurt utilized common sense in taking a simple spare tire and (figuratively – if not literally) beating his competition into non-factor status. To remove one's competition is the ultimate objective in sales. If we, as sales professionals, want to increase our closing ratios, increase our volume, increase our profits, and most importantly – increase our commissions, we would be wise to remember and emulate Kurt's "that cheap ol' temp tire" sales philosophy.

What "niche" does your product possess that makes it stand apart from the competition? Where is your competition vulnerable? What are your product's vulnerabilities (and is your competition using them against you?)? If you do not know – it would behoove you to find out.

Professional sales efficiency, in its purest form, is all about matching one's strengths against the weaknesses of the opponent; that is the field on which we need to play. However, when our opponents succeed in playing the game on their field (their strengths against our weaknesses), we will most likely lose if we do not have a strategy devised to counter, deflect, or negate (or at least marginalize) the perceived gap between their strengths and our weaknesses. The most effective game plan should always include our "niche!"

In salesmanship, we find "hot buttons" when we FIND AND DISPLAY "niches." It does absolutely no good to have a great "niche" if we fail to display it and utilize it strategically. Displaying the "niche" to our advantage should be part of a regular product presentation. At the most basic level of sales, what does our product do that no other product is capable of doing?

For years, I sold Volvos with a fellow salesperson named David who knew without a doubt what he needed to do in order to be successful selling Volvos. When contemplating the market's niches, he knew that his client would almost always purchase a Lexus ("bells and whistles"), or a BMW ("panache"), or a Mercedes ("prestige") if he let bells and whistles, panache, and/or prestige be elevated in importance to or above Volvo's strong point: safety! His strategy was simple and straightforward. "Sam, if you don't make them feel as if they're going to get killed if they buy something other than a Volvo – you're dead," he would frequently say. Obviously, it was a morbid (albeit effective) strategy. It worked for him! His entire sales presentation was about a steel safety cage, whiplash seats, ultra-high- strength steel to deter intrusion into the passenger compartments, torso airbags, crumple zones, and a myriad of safety data and statistics that would make any statistician proud. When doing their competitive comparisons, all consumers David worked with had to ultimately ask themselves, "Do I want "safety" or do I want "bells and whistles, panache, or prestige?" In the end, his statistics regarding "death rates" for Volvo versus the competition was compelling enough to cause a certain amount of angst at the local Lexus, BMW, and Mercedes dealerships. David won more battles than he lost. He did so by elevating his "niche" above the competition's "niche": in effect asking the question: "Do you want survivability in the event of a catastrophic accident – or would you prefer the latest electronic gadget - or to be the owner of a hood ornament that is the envy of your golfing buddies down at the local country club?" David was also not shy about letting his prospect know that gadgets and envy are short-lived; survivability, on the other hand, has a much longer shelf life (pardon the pun).

Our "niche" is most advantageous when it cannot be replicated by others. Many large corporations (Motorola, IBM, and Microsoft all know and pursue the advantages of exclusivity) seek the ability of their products and services doing what others cannot. They spend millions of dollars on research, patents, and trademarks in an effort to simply stand alone.

As sales professionals, we too stand alone when we find and display our "niches." The chances are good that your competition will not go to the trouble to find and display their "niche;" therefore, the chances are great that a salesperson who does not know his or her "niche" will be at a huge disadvantage to one who does – as it stands as the focal point of the entire sales process. Not surprisingly, when you find and utilize your "niche," you may not need a tiebreaker; nonetheless, it is nice to know it's in your back pocket just in case!

CHAPTER 14

RESOURCEFULNESS...
A STEP TO SUCCESS

"Even the most resourceful housewife cannot create miracles from a riceless pantry."

- Chinese Proverb

WHEN WE LOOK back throughout history, virtually all great leaders, pioneers, visionaries, scholars, coaches, inventors, and high-achieving business professionals utilized an assist from someone or something – or both. Very few people (if any) have achieved greatness in their professional endeavors by "going it alone" or through their sole intelligence, knowledge, wisdom, abilities, or work ethic. Typically, the "best" in most fields constantly seek out "a better way" by being open to (and intrigued by) the ideas and knowledge of others who have made significant contributions in their particular field.

Abraham Lincoln, for example, needed and utilized the abilities of Ulysses S. Grant to save not only the union – but ultimately the stature of his presidency as well. In fact, Lincoln once stated, "Tell me what brand of whiskey that Grant drinks. I would like to send a barrel of it to my other generals."

The most basic component of greatness is the sum generated by the input of self and others; the most basic component of failure is the sum generated by self. The old adage, "two heads are better than one" points us in the right direction to achieve success; however, it should also be noted that three heads may also be better than two in instances where the third head can add a contribution that the first and second heads could not.

Do we know how many "good" ideas it takes to make a "great" idea? How many "random" ideas does it take to make a "good" idea? Can ideas comingle to achieve a breakthrough or standard never before seen? Do two people from vastly differing backgrounds, working in tandem, have greater potential for achievement than one person working solo and through the prism of one narrow perspective? The singular answer to these questions, of course, is that no two situations or scenarios are exactly alike; hence, we must seek potential benefits, advancements, and solutions from as many areas as possible. Being resourceful is a mindset; the thought process is one in which the sheer volume of possibilities exponentially raises the potential for a favorable outcome as compared to the potential for a favorable outcome when possibilities are more limited.

Too often, people believe they are diminished when their efforts are part of a shared endeavor. It would be wise, however, to consider the great feats of not only legends, but their collaborators and cohorts as well. Would it have been possible for Vince Lombardi to have hoisted two Super Bowl trophies (later named the Vince Lombardi Trophy in his honor) if not for the efforts and abilities of Bart Starr, Ray Nitschke, Jerry Kramer, and/or his assistant coaches? Undoubtedly, Vince Lombardi knew he was one cog in molding the Green Bay Packers into world champions. As host of *The Johnny Carson Show*, was Johnny Carson diminished by sharing the stage with his sidekick Ed McMahon? Is Warren Buffet diminished when bouncing ideas off of Bill Gates (or vice versa)? Was Sonny Bono diminished by sharing a microphone with Cher? Dean Martin and Jerry Lewis were hysterically funny by themselves – but even funnier when paired together.

Successful people gravitate toward other successful people. Frequently, they draw ideas from each other – learn from each other – and inspire each other. Most importantly, successful people lift others up; unsuccessful people tend to de-motivate and tear others down. Our success (or lack of success) quite likely depends largely upon the company we keep. Our interactions and collaborations with other individuals are at the root of our ability to be resourceful to the extent it enhances our chances of attaining our goals and objectives.

A myriad of tools (other than people) also exists that can potentially enhance our productivity and efficiency. Many of those tools revolve around providing avenues from which we can communicate to and fro with potential, current, and past clients.

Snail- mail is largely considered to be antiquated in the twenty-first century; however, it does offer the element of surprise and shows a personal touch often lost in today's electronically-engaged society. The very idea that snail -mail is out of vogue elevates its status in the eyes of those who are chagrined by pop culture's dictation of "what's in vogue;" that percentage of individuals not being insignificant.

Being "different" and displaying "different" tendencies is not always a bad (or ineffective) thing! In professional sales, one of the most valuable resources we can utilize is that we are indeed "different;" we do not always adhere to conventional thought or wisdom. After all, how can we find a "better way" or a more productive way if we only do what others are doing? In simple terms, we sometimes step outside the norm to avoid mediocrity; we use what others will not use in order to be what others will not be and to do what others will not or cannot do.

Communicating on the Internet via e-mail is certainly embraced by the masses in today's business environment. Unquestionably, this method of communications offers several distinct advantages over snail-mail and other traditional methods of communications. Number one, it is more cost-effective than a stamp, envelope, and stationary. Number two, the benefits of the immediacy aspect cannot be denied in an era where "time is of the essence" has never been more essential. In today's business climate, using Internet communications is vital, and it is also a critical area that impacts the bottom line of any and every automotive dealership.

The key to using Internet communications effectively (and profitably) is to devise a strategy that addresses both what it can do for you (positively) and what it can do to you (negatively). From a negative and detrimental standpoint, in Internet communications, far too many sales professionals provide far too much information to prospective consumers online; so much information, in fact, that the prospective consumer has little need for walking through the doors of the dealership. The professional salesperson who thinks strategically, on the other hand, will provide only enough information to pique the interest of the prospective consumer in order to entice the prospect into the showroom (via creating a sense of urgency) sooner rather than later. Also, I have personally observed many sales professionals who have spent far too much time fully engaged with a screen as opposed to a live individual standing or sitting in front of them. Apparently, no one ever told these sales professionals that the Internet was a very good resource to supplement their sales goals and objectives: the operative word being SUPPLEMENT! In other words, the professional salesperson would be wise to view the Internet as icing on the cake. Unfortunately, I have seen many sales careers damaged (and monthly paychecks ruined) by sales associates who lose sight of the cake! In most simple terms, the icing will not (and cannot) pay our bills.

Over the course of the last fifteen years of my automotive sales career, I tried to place a greater emphasis upon the importance of resourcefulness than I did in the earlier stages of my fledgling career. I learned over time that doing one thing in one way was a recipe for one conclusion: average results. In the real world, average results equates to a modest paycheck and boatloads of frustration and stress. Trial and error provided me with feedback and results that indicated when I tried two or three things in two or three different ways, my paycheck was better, and my frustrations and stresses were lessened. The key is to mesh creativity and resourcefulness while maintaining consistency within the framework of our GAME PLAN!

During one frustrating period of slow sales, I repeatedly sent out flyers, notes, and letters to people I had spoken with (and been unable to sell) over the previous twelve months. I had literally sent out hundreds of envelopes with an enclosed reason that "NOW" was the time to get the best deal "EVER IN THE HISTORY OF THE WORLD" on a new vehicle. You can only imagine how emotionally drained I was when no one called, re-visited, or even acknowledged my very existence. I decided one day to try one more time – in a completely different way. Actually, the devil made me do it on a day I was vulnerable! It was rather devious – but a lot of fun because I thought it was humorous – and I was in need of some humor. Besides, my rationale was that the *^#@'s that had ignored me repeatedly deserved it. I went to the office stock room and brought back two boxes of envelopes. You could actually see a look on everyone's face in the dealership that simply said, "That stupid Sam's at it again – he never learns." I sat down and quickly addressed (by hand – and with atrocious handwriting) both boxes with the same names and addresses of the *^#@'s I had been bombarding for months. That afternoon, I sent both boxes of envelopes out in the afternoon mail with absolutely nothing inside the envelopes! Within days, the *^#@'s I had previously been 0 for 500 on were bombarding me with calls in bewilderment of what was missing from their envelope. Incredibly, I did sell several cars as a result of the unorthodox mailer! It also was the most effective mailer of my career in terms of opening up the lines of communication. Go figure!

The *^#@'s could not be enticed by offers of SALES, DISCOUNTS, GOOD DEALS, HOT DOGS, or appearances by THE DALLAS COWBOY CHEERLEADERS! An empty envelope with a thirty-cent stamp, however, did the trick. Creativity and resourcefulness require the realization that "one man's junk is another man's treasure."

There are innumerable ways in which we can pique the interest of our clientele. Undoubtedly, Abraham Lincoln's generals had their interest piqued when they received a barrel of Ulysses S. Grant's "brand of whiskey." In one's sales career, it may or may not be advisable to send clientele a "barrel of whiskey" or an empty envelope; however, it could be an effective strategy to "do what others do not – and do not what others do."

CHAPTER 15

PRESENTATION...
A STEP TO SUCCESS

"It takes one hour of preparation for each minute of presentation time."

- Wayne Burgraff

THE LADY BEHIND the cash register said, "Sir, would you like to save fifteen percent on your purchase today?" Immediately, my senses kicked in, and I was saved by my intuitiveness. "No thank you," spewed from my mouth without a moment's hesitation. My initial reaction was that a loaded question of that magnitude had to have been devised at the home office; I didn't want whatever it was the home office was selling. After all, if it was coming from the home office, it was a scheme to remove more money from my wallet. As I was pulling a twenty from my pocket, I overheard the lady at the next register ask her customer, "Sir, would you like to save fifteen percent on your purchase today?" The gentleman looked as if he was being chased by wild hyenas. I didn't hang around to hear the rest of the cashier's presentation; however, from the contorted look upon her prospect's face, she had a daunting task in front of her if she was to convince him the fifteen percent savings was tied to anything less than either selling his soul to the devil – or perhaps, applying for a credit card that would haunt him into eternity.

Obviously, the cashiers were simply doing what they had been ordered to do. The cashiers were not the morons; the brain trust at the home office who devised the question were the morons. Any question we ask or path we take that makes us look or feel stupid – and/or makes the consumer look or feel stupid is a poor business practice that is also ineffective more often than not. The small percentage of the time it is effective is not worth the ramifications that flow from insulting the intelligence of our clientele or our potential clientele.

Asking questions and making presentations in a manner showing respect for our product and also the intelligence of our clientele are major components of a sales process that should always be a win-win for both parties. We know from experience that superior sales professionals work toward an end result that produces a satisfied buyer and a satisfied seller.

Before we make important sales presentations (and personal presentations as well), it would be beneficial to consider the human psyche. The human being is a complex character; however, there are basic traits and motivators that apply on a widespread basis without regard to sex, race, national origin, or socioeconomic status. The two most dominant traits, as it relates to saying yes or no when one receives a proposal are: fear and motivation. In the sales process, fear of loss can be a huge motivator; as a result, a sense of urgency often results. Also, fear of the unknown can totally remove urgency from the equation – as no one wants to make a bad or uninformed decision that may have serious ramifications. Within the two seconds it took the cashier to ask me, "Sir, would you like to save fifteen percent on your purchase today?" a great fear of the unknown enveloped me as my mind searched for an answer to how much that fifteen percent savings was going to cost me over the long term. I am (as most people are) motivated by savings; however, I was more fearful of the ramifications than I was motivated by the fifteen percent savings. My immediate response was "NO!" Once I say NO, it is difficult to acquire a YES from me. It would require a total reevaluation of the situation, and I would need a comfort level that would necessitate the cashier suddenly becoming a certified counselor. Obviously, she did not (and I did not) have enough time for me to hang around while she received her psychiatric licensure.

When we make presentations, we most often are seeking a response of: YES. To acquire a YES, we would be most effective if we removed fear of the unknown as a factor in the decision-making process BEFORE we begin our presentation. How can that be accomplished? First and foremost, since many individuals are like myself in regard to the internal difficulties we struggle with as it relates to changing a NO to a YES, it might be wise to forego the attempt to get a YES or NO response during the early stages of a presentation. A better strategy could possibly be a simple statement such as, "Mr. Jones, I would like to make you aware of a benefit we are providing for our clientele – at this time." There are several advantages (for both parties) to this approach. Number one, we did not ask the customer for a commitment before he or she had enough facts to make an informed (and YES) decision. Number two, we piqued the interest of Mr. Jones with the word BENEFIT. Everyone likes benefits, and it does not formulate the aura of being trapped in the way SAVINGS does. At the conclusion of the statement, the wording AT THIS TIME places a sense of urgency upon the matter. In the sales process, it is much more to our advantage (from the seller's perspective) to interact with a prospect who feels a sense of urgency (fear of loss) as opposed to interacting with a prospect who feels angst and fear of the unknown. In the real world, the prospect who feels a sense of urgency (fear of loss) wants to hear more of what you have to say and offer; on the other hand, the prospect who feels the stress and fear of the unknown will be running for the door!

Ideally, a professional sales presentation should be executed with two objectives in mind. Number one, it is imperative to build enough value in our product or service to position it above the competition by illustrating benefits the competition does not (or cannot) provide. This, in effect, helps remove the competition from a potentially favorable status if the illustrated benefits are perceived by the consumer to be significant and/or desirable.

Highlighting stellar crash ratings, resale values, warranty advantages, dimension/specification differentials that provide performance benefits, and economic factors (i.e., fuel mileage ratings, cost of ownership, price, etc.) are a few logical prime targets where we may be able to "make hay" versus the competition when the prospect's analytical traits and self-interest tendencies are brought to the forefront.

Stimulating the consumer's analytical traits is a prelude to marrying those traits to his or her emotional traits. When the consumer can touch it, feel it, smell it, see it, and bask in it – we, as sellers, find ourselves in a much more strategically – enhanced position than that of our competition who may fail to realize the importance of stimulating the analytical and emotional traits of the consumer.

All too often, consumers walk through the doors of dealerships and fervently vow that the only color acceptable is blue. All too often, as well, sales associates (in touch with the consumer's fervency – and realizing he or she does not have a "blue" in stock) walk the consumer to a desk and begin the process of ordering or dealer-transferring a "blue one" to meet the desires of his or her client. In this scenario, the salesperson is bypassing the emotional traits of his or her prospect and allowing the analytical traits to supersede the emotional ones. This is nothing short of sales malpractice. The sales professional who walks the inventory with his or her prospect in search of a "blue one" (even though he or she knows it doesn't exist in the inventory) will often be pleasantly surprised to see the prospect drooling over a "red one" five minutes after he or she said "blue" was the only color that would suffice. In effect, the professional salespersons who take one more step (beyond the analytical) are frequently rewarded with a sale that resulted from emotional traits rising above and prevailing over analytical traits.

There is a reason that five-star restaurants place as much emphasis upon ambiance as they do food. It is not impossible to get fifty bucks for a twenty- five dollar steak if the lighting is dim, the music plays ever-so-softly, and the waiter speaks with a hint of an accent. Restaurants with sage managers never offer chicken on the menu; they offer Chicken Cordon Bleu. Wise professionals in the hospitality industry realize there is more money (and more profitability) in the business of ambiance than in the business of food; therefore, the food (an essential element of a restaurant) is coupled with the ambiance (a nonessential element of operations – yet, an essential element of desired profitability).

Do those of us in the automotive industry simply peddle sheet metal – or do we create ambiance? Are we more productive (and provide a better and more professional experience for the consumer) when we remove the vehicle from the inventory so the prospect can visualize it as it stands alone? Do we take the extra step of tuning the stereo to a channel that most likely fits the demographics of our consumer? Rap doesn't provide much ambiance for seventy-five year olds in most cases! Do we take one extra minute and heat or cool the vehicle (as appropriate to weather conditions) while we allow the consumer to wait inside and enjoy a cup of coffee? Do we take the time to make sure the vehicle we are showing has an adequate amount of gas? In the winter, do we turn the heated seats on before the potential client sits his or her derriere in the driver's seat? In the end, do we show our clientele consideration and the respect they deserve?

I never order chicken when I can order Chicken Cordon Bleu. I never buy blue when I can have Tango Red. I will never buy leather seats if I can invest in "Corinthian leather."

My analytical traits will allow me to purchase a good value. My emotional traits will make me pay twice as much for exquisite chocolates – as opposed to chocolates. It's all in the presentation!

CHAPTER 16

BODY LANGUAGE…
A STEP TO SUCCESS

"I speak two languages, Body and English."

- Mae West

IN A SALES environment, it is not uncommon for a prospective buyer to say one thing verbally and something entirely different with nonverbal communications. In these instances, body language is a far better indicator than oral communications as it relates to what the individual is truly thinking and feeling.

A perceptive sales professional pays closer attention to what people tell him or her with their eyes, hands, postures, and facial expressions than with their lips. Very few people have the ability, concentration, and mental discipline to consistently align verbal output with nonverbal indicators when the verbal output is false, misleading, or inaccurate.

Professional sales representatives would be well served to clearly understand the basics of two-way communications from two vantage points; number one, the nonverbal signals being sent from the prospective buyer to the seller – and equally important, the nonverbal signals being sent from the seller to the prospective buyer.

For the most effective two-way communications to take place, both parties need nonverbal assurances that the dialogue is accurate. In the real world, both parties are simply trying to determine whether or not the other party is being "straight" with them. In two-way communications, once accuracy is detected by both parties, there is a greater likelihood of visible signs indicating comfort and trust; arms once folded become more relaxed, eye contact begins to take place, and fidgeting and/or erratic movements with the hands dissipates. Greater eye contact and stability with the hands are co-indicators that nervousness has lessened and trust has increased; both are necessities for a fruitful and productive transition from the initial stages of the sales process to the negotiating stage.

Attempting to negotiate a transaction before trust has been established (and clearly visible) is a surefire recipe for nonproductive negotiations; often such negotiations deteriorate into chaos or delay – either or both being a "kiss of death" for the completion of a successful and profitable transaction.

When confronted with conflicting communication signals from one's prospect, the astute sales professional can often find new levels of mutual openness and trust by suspending the active stages of the sales process and leading the prospect to an area (physically and/or emotionally) less stressful and/or less focused upon the business aspects of the dialogue; a transition more focused upon commonalities shared by both parties. In other words, a wise sales professional will retreat to the building rapport and finding common ground stage when faced with an untenable communications obstacle that will prove difficult to overcome if he or she plows forward. Once the verbal and nonverbal become aligned, the sales professional can reignite the sales process (from where it was suspended) in a more productive manner.

In the execution of our daily business interactions, when we cross paths with someone who will not look us in the eye, fidgets while we converse, keeps their arms crossed in a defensive and closed posture, and/or gives us a "dead fish" handshake, it is tempting to dismiss the individual as a "flake" or someone who is weak or lacking in character. Many individuals, however, are simply unaware of the signals they are sending with their body language; as a result, their true feelings (angst, fear of the unknown, apprehension, etc.) are on full display. As sales professionals, we need to constantly remind ourselves that it isn't the responsibility of the consumer to make us feel comfortable or "sell us" on their individual merits and strengths. It is, however, our responsibility (to ourselves and our employer) to turn discomfort into comfort, fear into calmness, uncertainty into confidence, and negatives into positives. In and of itself, this is the very essence of salesmanship!

In the early stages of my sales career, I once had the pleasure of working with the best communicator one could ever imagine. His name was Rodney; everybody loved Rodney. Not only did everybody love Rodney – they loved him immediately. Bankers loved Rodney; bricklayers loved Rodney. Young people loved Rodney; old people loved Rodney. Women loved Rodney immensely; men loved him instinctively.

Every man who came in contact with Rodney suddenly had a best friend; Rodney was king of the "man-crush." It is also important to note that Rodney had a closing ratio that was off the charts. Rodney did not make very many "Ya did!" phone calls. If one of Rodney's customers did not buy from him – it was a safe assumption that the prospect's credit was in the tank, or they had so much negative equity in their trade that it would have taken Jacques Cousteau and an underwater expedition to once again get their head above water.

I once heard a story about the CEO of Rolex dining at a fine restaurant. An acquaintance walked by and patted him on the back and asked, "How's the watch business?" The CEO reacted with uncertainty and confusion, "I don't know," he said. The acquaintance responded, "How can you not know how the watch business is – you're the CEO of Rolex?" The CEO stated, "I'm not in the watch business – I'm in the people business!"

Well, there you have it. The great ones (Rodney and the Rolex CEO) aren't in the watch business – or the car business – or the real estate business – or the financial services business. They're in the "people" business!

I have never seen anyone better at the "people" business than Rodney. He made everyone he came in contact with feel better about that moment in time – and themselves. He could relate to people (not through his words – but in the way he interacted with them) in a manner that few can. After five minutes of interaction, if I laid hands on people the way Rodney did, I would get arrested. Rodney, on the other hand, got an invitation to dinner.

Rodney used humor and good-naturedness to lighten the mood. When he laughed with his customer, he grabbed their left forearm with his left hand, patted them on the upper left shoulder and shook his entire body as they laughed together. It wasn't sexual or romantic; it was fraternal. When a person laughed with Rodney, they not only saw and heard his laugh, they felt his laugh (and vice versa). In a nutshell, Rodney built his customer's self-esteem; in so doing, his customer's would have preferred admitting cheating on their spouse on national television than to call Rodney and tell him they had bought a car from another salesman. He worked hard to attain their trust – and he was often rewarded with their loyalty.

The most basic element of Rodney's repertoire was the way he made people feel "SPECIAL!" His sole focus while working with an individual was THAT individual; he did not allow himself to be distracted by outside forces. Even though it was an era before cell phones, Rodney would have been aghast at the very thought of taking (or making) a call while working with a consumer. In today's society, where cell phones (and other electronic devices) are a pacifier and a rampant addiction to large segments of the public, sales representatives (and dealerships) forfeit massive amounts of income by being undisciplined in cell phone usage; make no mistake, it is a common occurrence that impacts the bottom line to an incalculable degree. To put it bluntly, the salesperson who takes a call while working with a prospect (provided it is not a matter of death, birth or grave injury) is an idiot! To do so makes a huge negative statement to one's prospect (You're unimportant!). Show me a salesperson who receives and makes calls during any aspect of the sales process, and I will show you a salesperson with a low closing ratio and low earnings. Not only does such indifference transmit a negative message, it also disrupts the crucial 4F's of sales: focus, flow, fervency, and formula. Since all F's of the 4F's are intertwined, we lose the benefits of all when we lose the benefit of one. In essence, when we lose focus, we also lose flow, fervency, and formula (and any combination thereof).

Positive momentum is a crucial aspect of any sales process. When we sabotage the benefits we have derived from the 4F's, the prospect is provided with an "out" that he or she can utilize to terminate or "delay" the sales process. When the sales process arrives at this junction, the consumer is in total control – and the salesperson has zero control. A wise sales professional never provides his or her prospect with an "out" or an avenue by which control can be transferred from seller to buyer. When we are fortunate enough to be engaged in the sales process with a consumer, it would behoove us to look upon our cell phones as "out" phones. The costs, in unrealized income, of using "out" phones (to salespersons and dealerships) is, undoubtedly, exorbitant. Personally, I cannot afford to take (or make) those calls; whether or not you can afford to use an "out" phone is your decision.

We have all heard the adage, "It isn't what you say – it's how you say it." In professional sales, being cognizant of the entire aura surrounding human interactions is critical to our effectiveness in ultimately closing the deal. I offer one piece of advice (via Rodney and the Rolex CEO) to those who seek success in professional sales: Get in the "people" business!

It is difficult for a professional who gets in the "people" business to fail; conversely, it is difficult for one who only gets in the "product" business to succeed.

CONCLUSION

The retail automotive industry is a tough gig in the best of times and under the best of circumstances. Unfortunately, these times and circumstances no longer exist. Before we can thrive, we must first survive the realities and obstacles that have permeated the automotive industry.

Having a GAME PLAN is the only thing that can save us. If we "go about business as usual," we are destined for extinction. In short, we must "do what others don't – and don't what others do."

The masses in "the car business" continue to utilize the SEVEN STEPS TO THE SALE methodology which has been used for decades. This methodology has produced mediocrity and "average results" on a widespread and consistent basis. We must go beyond that which has not worked and will never work.

To find consistency and extraordinary levels of success, we must be a student of failure and success; we must find common ground with our clientele at a deeper level and create a sense of urgency. We must mesh knowledge with an expansive imagination; we must find our niches and always assume the sale. To reiterate, we must "do what others don't – and don't what others do."

Most importantly, we must always be looking for "the angel in the marble." We must always "carve until we set him free."

ACKNOWLEDGEMENTS

I wish to say "thank you" to two of the best educators in America. These two individuals gave *SIXTEEN STEPS TO $IX-FIGURE$: A GAME PLAN FOR SALES SUCCESS* its life and structure. Walters State Community College should be exceedingly proud of Barbara McNeely and Sherri Mahone Jacobs. Again, thank you Barbara and Sherri!

www.ingramcontent.com/pod-product-compliance
Lightning Source LLC
Chambersburg PA
CBHW022015170526
45157CB00003B/1250